The Publicist's Playbook

CHAPTERS

1

INTRODUCTION TO A WORLD OF FINITE POSSIBILITIES

I really didn't want to start a book about public relations with a quote about advertising. But here we are because sometimes you illustrate what *is* by pointing out what *isn't*.

Many readers will be familiar with the tired old line that advertising is 'the most fun you can have with your clothes on'. Public relations, on the other hand, is a career for inquisitive, world-aware individuals who are 'interested in being interested'. PR is cerebral. It would have to be because words are amongst our only tools, whereas the other side of town, Advertising, has full-colour, live and direct, 3D everything in HD.

If you think PR is all parties, you're getting confused with Eventing, PR's better-looking cousin who does a good job disguising the fact that she's a lot of hard work. This book is primarily about PR of the press release and social media content variety, perhaps with a dash of press conferencing tossed in for good measure. I should mention that the latter are all tools of the trade because what's really important in PR is achieving good, old-fashioned media coverage. Acres and acres of online and print media space, and hours of sound-bites, are the goals of any respectable PR person who is not out to bullshit his client with long-winded strategies and PR waffle. If you're not achieving media coverage for your client, then you're simply not doing your job as a PR consultant.

Interpersonal relationships, and tips for making them easier and more effective, are also included in this book. This is because PR consultants couldn't get anything published without relying on people to do the publishing. And lest we forget, clients are people too!

When it comes to traditional PR, forget the ad industry fun mentioned above. Well-deserved fun with friends you can earn after-hours following a 10-hour day. I can promise you PR won't be too much fun early in the game when you haven't yet earned the stripes necessary to enjoy long lunches in swanky places. Instead, you'll be the one tasked with updating awfully long media distribution lists through endless, eye-straining Googling, or awkward phone conversations with journalists who believe you should already have their phone number - after all, you called them… Fortunately, photocopying phonebook-thick black and white print publicity reports has largely died a well-deserved death, except in the most obscure PR firms in the most remote Appalachian towns, I presume.

The bit about fun above notwithstanding, being fortunate enough to work within a professional PR outfit has one standout advantage over agency life in most other marketing-related industries. You'll be exposed to people and events you would never usually have been fortunate enough to interact with, had you chosen a one-dimensional profession. The bright young account manager, for example, will get to speak with a lot more leading minds across so many varied industries compared with her similarly-aged peers in other jobs. Obviously, this is dependent on a particular agency's client list.

If I think of my own example, I've not only been introduced to a President of South Africa, had tea with Winston Churchill's grandson (late, now), arranged radio and television interviews for Marty Cooper (Motorola's inventor of the first true cellphone), and interviewed Dan Bahat (chief archaeologist for the city of Jerusalem), but I've met a ton of interesting people besides. I've loved the fact that my own generally optimistic nature has been complemented by my career in PR where I've helped publicise some truly inspiring corporate social responsibility projects that have made me hopeful for the future.

Many PR books seem to be advertorials for their authors and their PR firms, so I'll stop there. The purpose of this book is not to be a record of anyone's PR career. I wanted it to be interesting, with some humour to keep your attention up, and generally littered with plenty of actual hints and tips that you can implement successfully in your own career.

What this book isn't is a PR textbook. When I was researching PR books prior to writing this one, I was disappointed to see that each seemed to wind along the same old route. The introduction would chug along for page after uninspiring page about what PR is, providing multiple definitions from irrelevant PR bodies that do nothing for illustrating what exactly it is that PR people do all day. Then there are the vanity projects, alluded to above, where the reader is endlessly exposed to the author's own PR awesomeness.

There are a limited number of things you need to know in PR. I realised this after sitting in status meeting after status meeting and hearing the same limited box of tricks being pulled out for every client. The fact that there is only so much you can do as a PR person doesn't discount the profession. I mean, what does a surgeon do but cut?

What this finite realm of PR possibility meant to me was the realisation that I need to write this stuff down. So I started making notes a few years ago whenever I did something I thought would interest other PR people, especially the younger ones who might not yet have experienced the benefits of being exposed to all sides of the PR business. These include working in an agency, gravitating to a client's Corporate Affairs department, eventually starting one's own agency, and then going it alone as a consultant with an assistant.

The "Publicist's Playbook" is about introducing the reader to all the lessons I learnt along the way in an engaging manner, being careful always to keep things tangible and easily implementable in the reader's own environment. The targets of this book are account-facing employees within PR firms, employees working within corporate PR departments, PR firm owners looking for additional insights, and students looking for real-world PR information.

A short note about gender issues: please be assured that using 'he', 'his' and 'him' in no way minimises the equally brilliant work done by 'she', 'hers' and 'her' – for brevity it's simply easier to use one gendered pronoun. Any offence taken by overly-prickly types can be rapidly put into perspective with a flick of the remote control to view what's going down in the world that's substantively unrelated to pronouns.

Now let's get on with it.

2

MAN BITES NEWS, NEWS BITES DOG...?

The steady demise of the hardcopy newspaper has had several unforeseen consequences. The venerable art of folding a broadsheet into quarters while balancing a G&T on one's knee will soon be lost forever. Holes cannot easily be cut in the centre of tablets, seriously impacting national security. And many people in PR jobs today can't correctly answer this erstwhile easy question:

News is:

A) The CEO's 50th birthday
B) What old people talk about
C) A million dollars spent on a local procurement drive
D) Two million dollars spent on team-building

News is what used to be important enough to make it onto a printed page. Because there are tight space constraints associated with printed pages, compared to the virtually unlimited capacity of cyberspace, you could be sure that what made it onto that folded broadsheet page you were reading was the real deal. It certainly wasn't this crap from CNN.com:

"Greenland sharks, which live an average of at least 272 years, rank as the longest-lived vertebrates on Earth, a new study indicates; they may live beyond 400 years."

Can you imagine this comma-studded shocker appearing as an opening line in a hardcopy FT story? The content is interesting, the way it is composed is disgraceful. I've come to the heart of the matter. Online news websites are littered with editing errors. That's not the worst of it. The worst is that an obvious error from years back will remain on an online news platform without ever being corrected.

I used to tell my account managers to go downstairs and buy a copy of Business Day from the corner shop to see how news is supposed to be written. The funny thing now is even if the newspaper were still available, it's the corner shop that's missing! Today, we have to enter a horribly over-lit garage shop to buy the few remaining hardcopy titles. And to suffer shattered eardrums at 7am, as the barista has replaced George behind the counter and it's not his job to ask about the kids. His job is to make average coffee at a premium price.

The dominance of online media platforms that don't prioritise punchy, well-written stories that answer the traditional what, where, when, who and why in the opening paragraph - because they are hardly subject to space constraints - means that a whole PR generation is used to writing sloppy copy with no clear news angle and getting away with it. Bad media parents have raised bad PR children, and now journalists are wondering why they receive press releases that wind on remorselessly like a Fidel Castro speech without ever getting to the point.

For our purposes, news can be divided into hard news that's definitely going to make it into quality online platforms and hardcopy editions, and iffy corporate news that's got an OK shot at being published. I'm calling the latter 'iffy' news because it might be published IF you can present it correctly in a well-written press release that links it to some, more important news of the day. It might also be published IF you can get journalists to notice you because you took the trouble to compose an introductory email that summarises the news angle you're taking.

Hard news is 'Hitler Invades Poland'. It's serious stuff. Today, because the world has fallen in love with commerce and industry, products and services; what corporations are doing matters. This means PR people like you and me have a real chance of getting our clients and employers into the media. Fifty years ago, who would write about 'girl children' ('girls', perhaps?) being taken to work?

The fact that journalists are even talking to PR people - sometimes even as equals - is a tremendous opportunity for you. Just remember that you still need to link your corporate news to some wider news issue to receive exposure. That's (usually) even true with dodgy 'news' sites that will publish anything just to get numbers up for their future corporate advertising proposals. Link your small news to some other big news and write smiley emails with no spelling errors to journalists, and you should be a for away!.

Something that almost skipped my mind is the value of external PR consultants. Funny that. Look how Mr Booth has made a living, yet he forgets to punt his own lot. When people work for large companies, they can sometimes get so caught up in the internal whirlwind - especially when there is a charismatic CEO - that they fail to appreciate that most of what the organisation is doing is simply of no interest to anyone. An external PR consultant can help you appreciate just how insignificant your company is. Surely saving face is a wonderful reason to hand over a retainer every month?

In conclusion, it's 'C'. The answer is 'C'!

3

WRITING IS FOR THE Bs

Writing is a skill that can be polished with practice. That's a huge bit of good fortune for you because you're very likely going to need solid writing skills if you're going to rub out the PR competition. But the bad news is that your education that prioritised knowledge over knowing is not going to help much when you confuse *your* with *you're*.

Let's stop predictable diaper-bashing for a moment and clarify why PR people need good writing skills. The thing is, many don't, actually. You get to the top of the PR game by being either a worker or an operator. A worker is like me. I've always been behind my keyboard, knocking out real written work that requires a bit of time and some intellect. When I first entered the corporate world, I thought studiously remaining in my office on the second floor working away was the thing to do when the competition was swanning around the executive wing. I also liked stringing words together in interesting new ways. So worker bee it was.

This brings me to the operators. Operators know how to schmooze and are never to be found at their desks. Their skill is not producing great content that will eventually achieve the publicity we all assume is our goal. Their skill is knowing who to rub up and how.

That's because operators are all about publicising themselves. They're not interested in headlines mentioning their employer, or client. In fact, one operator I know was notorious for the early morning sweep-through where she would enter the office in a big performance and never sully her paws with the acres of newsprint lying a metre from her desk. Her - smart - modus operandi was to get to the office early and immediately transport herself to the executive suite where she would, quite simply, make her presence known. The rest of the morning was devoted to her own proprietary blend of delegation and general interference in anything connected with the letters C, E & O.

She wasn't a do-er, she was a talker, and she talked exceptionally well. Did she need to know the difference between *your* and *you're*? Of course not. She had the worker bees for such trifling details. There is nothing wrong with this, let me be clear on that.

In PR, you either write well or you schmooze well. Some gifted people can do both. That's their good fortune. But the great news for the rest of us, is that a profitable PR career and indeed, PR business, can be built by both the worker bee writer and the operator schmoozer. You just need to be honest with yourself, figure out what you're about, and hire or outsource the skills you're lacking. There's an additional tactic you can choose: you can fine-tune what skills you already have through regular practice.

This brings me back to the need to write well, and if not well, then passably. To be honest, unless you're sending stories to the likes of The Economist, passably should do. Editors and journalists have always been used to receiving garbage, so if you can write a couple notches above garbage then you're doing better than most. I shudder to say it, but speed is what really impresses employers and clients these days. They just want something from you, in their inbox, this afternoon. If you can push out two notches above garbage, twice as fast, you've won.

This is how you write passably well, really fast. You first read so many news websites, regularly, that you become the only person actually avoided by the local opinionated barfly. This is because your outstanding general knowledge means he can't mouth off around you without being challenged. Your knowledge also becomes a wonderful internal press release resource. You'll be able to receive a brief, settle down in front of your keyboard, and start writing copy right away while your colleagues are still wasting time surfing the web searching for an angle, a quotable quote or some opening statistic.

After years spent searching the web for press release content which I thought would impress the client and the media, I've realised that while research does have a place, it's time that matters. You cannot afford to spend ages looking for random stuff to include in your releases and opinion articles. The random stuff should be stored in your head. It's quicker to retrieve that way, and if one too many client bonding sessions has made your memory fuzzy, then you can always fact-check using the web.

So, sit down, open the document editor and resist the temptation to click on the Internet icon. The second step is to devote the most time to the headline and the opening paragraph. You should spend 80 percent of the 30 to 40 minutes it should take to write a decent press release ensuring that the headline and the first paragraph read as though they were written in 30 seconds by Pulitzer himself. Smooth. Seamless. Flow. These are words that matter here.

My experience is that journalists will fix up the lesser paragraphs but if they can't see a news angle through the clutter of a lazy headline and a badly-composed opening paragraph, the story won't get used. Once you've finished these two, read them again and again, each time removing any unnecessary words. Once you're down to the bare bones necessary to get the crux of the message across, write the next (and last) 300 or so words.

Don't delay by planning paragraphs. Give it all a cursory read through just to check for any obvious spelling and grammar errors. Anything majorly wrong will be picked up by the clients, and they want to be able to send to you a few easy changes because they're on the clock too, and can't afford to waste time on PR.

Some people write entire books about constructing the perfect release. That's a good revenue spinner for them, but totally over the top for you. In time, with enough practice and using your general knowledge, as well as information supplied by the client, you'll be able to knock out concise press releases that are readable and get you plenty of media hits.

Practice will take care of any inherent flaws in your writing DNA. Oh, and fear of your nasty boss or a particularly hectic client. How could I forget that terrified account executives outperform happy account executives by a factor of three to one? I found that on the Internet.

4

PRESS RELEASE WRITER, MASTER CONTENT CREATION!

When current or potential clients ask whether you manage social media, in addition to "writing press releases", answer affirmatively because regardless of your actual level of proficiency in social media, you can learn.

Social is easy. Just look at the clowns doing it and I don't mean the US President. In fact, I really don't mean The Donald because - actually - and regardless of whether you like him or not, he really has shown many of us how one can indeed communicate directly with audiences, without intermediaries, for better or for worse. You can also fix your own pipes, but it doesn't mean you won't have a terrible flood later on.

At the end of the day, you need only figure out the four most important social platforms: Facebook, Twitter, Instagram (debatable for business - seriously) and LinkedIn. It's easy enough to surmise that 80% of operational PR people who either work for themselves, within corporate PR departments or for an agency, will only ever use these four platforms.

Of course, there are others. More will be added next year and the year after that. However, for all intents and purposes, if you can recite the names of the big four social platforms in your next client pitch, you'll be credited with knowing what you're talking about. Operationally, posting social updates that look passable is a breeze. With a little bit of practice after Googling the basics, you'll manage and you'll be great within a couple weeks.

Now more than ever, clients are looking for value in retainers and you absolutely must include at least a limited social media set within your PR service offering. If you don't, your client will be tempted to sign with those ad guys in the trendy part of town who said they could manage PR and do social to boot! Who wouldn't go for the three-in-one special?

The problem is that PR depends on writing, and in fact, social does too. So who better to handle both than the original "press release writer"?

You need to impress upon the client that a PR person can do media relations really well, and social media passably well. Advertising practitioners and social specialists - on the other hand - can do social really well but media relations very badly. Don't allow your clients to be bullshitted into three-in-one specials, and don't allow yourself to be bullied by ridiculously-hip looking ad and social people who are all smoke and mirrors, no substance.

Writing is best left to writers, and design is best left to the creatives. Content is the current buzzword, and you must hammer home to your clients that PR people have been doing content all along. After all, it's we who have been coming up with great angles to sell to journalists for years. It's we who have been turning those clever angles into well-written press releases for years. And the press release is the granddaddy of all content written by anyone who isn't a journalist, surely?

Make sure that your client, and anyone on the marketing team, whether internal employee or external consultant, understands that content creation should be the preserve of public relations.

Tell him you'll craft beautifully-written press releases that are the natural starting point of the content creation journey. Suggest that based on your extensive understanding of current affairs and newsworthiness, you're best placed to draft that initial press release on which Advertising, Social and the client can comment and approve.

You can then commit to pulling out two to three tweets from each release for Twitter; you can furthermore promise a 50-word Facebook status update or two, as well as summarising the typically 400-word press release into a 200 word LinkedIn article.

Given your intimate understanding of what's news and what's not, you can even throw in a commitment to produce short video question-and-answer interviews with the client based on the 'quotable quotes' within the press release for additional social platforms like YouTube, Vimeo or Vine, amongst others. A smartphone's the only video camera you'll need. Order a cellphone tripod online and a pull-up banner complete with your client's logo to really knock it (cost-effectively) out of the ballpark.

Finally, tell all gathered around the client's boardroom table for that weekly status meeting with the advertising agency and other external consultants, that you'll also prepare a short caption using the press release copy, and find an awesome visual to go with it for Instagram.

That's how PRs make themselves relevant in the age of Social. We've spent decades successfully fighting off the ad agencies who wanted to take our business. Social media consultants are just the latest mini-threat to drop into the corporate swamp with a ton of pie chart-based bullshit. Your writing is your strength, so show them how it's done.

5

PR STRATS: REALLY AWESOME ANGLES & DON'T FORGET SOCIAL

About two out of every ten clients have ever stuck to the PR strategy I prepared at the start of our relationship.

That's precisely why I have always suspected the PR strategy document is like the degree certificate hanging on many of our walls. The details are not important. You've only proved that you have what it takes to successfully surmount this obstacle placed in front of you. And that is reason enough to choose you over the next person. Being able to draft a strategy document well enough so that it looks like it ticks all the required PR boxes is simply a rite of passage to be welcomed into the world of press releases and fixed monthly retainers.

Most clients forget all about the PR strategy you drafted as soon as the first media success appears, because that first hit proves to them you know what you're doing. However, I have noticed that some clients will whip out that hitherto forgotten strategy document at contract renewal time and point to what was, in fact, mutually-agreed amnesia as some sort of retainer fee bargaining tool. So be wary of dispensing with strategies completely, even with client consent.

The strategy does actually serve something resembling a purpose – how, you may ask? Well, in that seeing story angles, targeted media, timelines and the terms and conditions of your relationship set out in a formal document helps ensure both PR firm are PR client are, quite literally, on the same page. Strategies are useful, then, because any glaring disconnect can be spotted early on. Beyond that, I've found them a colossal waste of time that prevent us from getting on with the only important PR task, and that's generating media coverage. Or preventing it, if you're a tobacco company, or similarly engaged in spectacular wrongdoing.

The above notwithstanding, while the drafting of the PR strategy is indeed a bit of a hoop-jumping exercise, you will still need to come up with something that will impress the client enough to hire you. Prove to the prospective client that you know what you are doing by making sure your PR strategy includes the following:

- While keeping the strategy short, reference as many media outlets as possible, and include the names and titles of specific journalists. Do not only refer to vague media categories like 'Business', 'Consumer', etc. Details impress clients. They need to see names, names, names! You need to prove you know who's who in the media zoo.

- While cutting and pasting vast tracts from previous client strategies is perfectly acceptable because we shouldn't be reinventing the wheel - in the interests of productivity - make doubly sure you remove all references to any other client company names. It's horribly embarrassing to spot another client's name when you're going through what was supposed to be a bespoke strategy with your prospective new client.

- Testimonials from other happy clients are worth their weight in gold because you can use the best ones year after year. Always keep a lookout in your inbox for great one-liner compliments from clients. If you spot a really nicely-phrased one from a client, ask his permission to use it in pitches and collect these short testimonials in a separate file. If you have really close relationships with a few well-known journalists, you could ask them if they'd mind receiving an email now and again from your potential clients. Including respected journalists in your list of references should go a long way towards impressing would-be clients. It's doubtful they would email, but the association with that top-notch media name is what you want.

- The best way to prove that you know what makes news, and are therefore the client's best choice of PR partner, is to come up with a list of convincing story angles to include in your strategy. Listing original story angles no one else has ever thought of and that can be developed into press releases, opinion articles, case studies, letters to the editor, blog posts, interview motivations and more, also proves that your strategy is more than just a cut and paste job. It will also prove that you've put some thought into what exactly it is you'll be doing content-wise for the client every week. You need to also include the targeted media, as awesome angles are no good without the accompanying platform on which they'll likely feature. I've realised over the years that it is the creativity of your story angles that seals the PR deal for the client.

- Clients are keen to know what exactly it is you'll be doing for them on a regular basis. This means including as much detail about real, on-the-ground PR tactics as possible. Aside from the writing side of PR, you'll need to include such PR tactic examples as hosting media lunches, support during press conferences and product launches, limited in-house media monitoring, the managing of exclusives, delivering product samples, etc.

- PR strategies these days can never just be media strategies. You must integrate social media into your plan or risk losing out to the ad agency that says it can include PR and social under an advertising strategy umbrella. The best way to do this is to emphasize your quality writing, unique story angles and extensive media contacts. Due to this latter triple whammy, you can then make it clear that PR is best placed to inform content creation across all non-paid platforms, whether they be media platforms or social media platforms.

6

STOP THE PRESS CONFERENCE

PR tools include the much-discussed press release and the overused press conference. The PR consultant can also whip out an array of lunchtime reservations, gift cards and giveaways to get the job done and the story squashed or placed, as the client may dictate. But for now, let's cast the spotlight on the PR golden child: the press conference.

Popular culture in the form of astonishingly over-the-top, media-themed TV shows - and Donald Trump's Twitter account - would have us believe that press conferences are heady, glamorous affairs called often and at the drop of a hat. The truth is in there somewhere, but we need to find and expose it.

Although the venue can add some shine, press conferences are usually more boring than glittering. They can indeed be scheduled at the last minute (usually when something awful happens), and they can be well-attended, but things have gotten so crazy and competitive in traditional and social media that hosted events like press conferences, media briefings and product launches just mean time out of the office for busy journalists and bloggers who are in a perpetual 'race to place'.

The first one to write the story, and get it up on the site, wins. The media opinion makers of today cannot afford to engage in any activity that does not get them an impression or click-generating story really quickly. Battling traffic and looking for parking is firmly within the realm of useless, non-productive activities. Yes, there are investigative journalists who take weeks, months or even years to research and write once-in-a-lifetime, award-wining pieces of work, and they'll clock up the miles, but these are usually not the type of media the PR wants around their client. They're the type of journalist who sees the cloud in every silver lining and who can be counted on to affect a jaded countenance quite at odds with the year-end party to which they've erroneously been invited by someone soon to quit.

By the way, you're under no obligation to invite any journalist to a press conference who is going to make your life difficult. You're not in government. You're helping promote, probably, a profit-making commercial concern, and you don't have to give anyone the opportunity or ammunition they require to trash the client who pays your invoices. Tell the truth, always, but don't go out there dishing out easy ways for the naysayers to damage your client's organisation. If people want to make your life difficult, do the same to them.

Some clients are very fond of hosting press conferences. This is usually because they are pursuing some other agenda like their own careers, and they are in need of a shiny platform paid for by their employer of the month. This is kind of fine, except when their perpetual calling of press conferences starts resulting in very thin media attendance as journalists realise that attending your client's vanity parades does nothing to fill blank screen space.

When a client first suggests calling a press conference, suggest back that you could probably achieve the same level of media exposure with a well-written press release emailed with an accompanying photo, logo, infographic or some other eye-catching visual to illustrate the story. Emphasize, especially to smaller clients funded by the founder, that you'll be able to get exposure this way at a much lower cost. Plus, mention that instead of relying on a few journalists to rock up in the flesh and get the news out, you could simply email the press releases to your extensive media distribution list and achieve much more bang per buck.

Simultaneously offering each contact a follow-up phone or Skype call with the client, to explore his own angle, would be like talking to individual journalists at the sidelines of an actual press conference, with added convenience. *Not* hosting a press conference, preferring instead to limit information to a selection of approved words in a short press release, also means much greater control over what is eventually published.

A cost-effective and more controllable alternative to the press conference is the hosting of sequential one-on-ones with the media most important to your client. This simply means, for example, inviting individual journalists to each interview the client for, say, 45 minutes, with 15-minute breaks in between to allow the client to recharge a little.

The venue is typically the comfortable lobby of a business hotel or a large, upscale restaurant that everybody knows. Ideally, you don't want the attending journalists to know other media people have been invited to chat with the client that morning. The trick is for the PR person to appear at the end of each 45-minute slot to gently usher each journalist to his car (don't forget the paid parking ticket) with a joke and a thank you before the next person appears.

When it comes to the formal press conference, why would you allow your client to open himself up to uncontrolled cross-examination - in public? The publicist's mind boggles. Leave press conferences to major, bad news events. Less newsworthy, good news belongs in a press release and everybody prefers it that way.

Here are a few pointers for when the press conference is unavoidable, and name tag holders and Brother label machines must be dusted off:

- It's not just about the press. Inviting selected bloggers, leading social media influencers and other worthy personalities says to the market your client is in step with current media trends and understands that journalists are not the only opinion makers.

- Start the press conference on time and at a specific time. It's no longer necessary to state times as, say, 09h00 for 09h15. This wastes precious minutes and annoys those valuable early birds. Give an exact time. Make sure you don't only rely on email, but also use social media, if appropriate, to remind those invited of your press conference.

- If the press conference is set to be a substantial affair, or the news is applicable to a number of time zones and territories, you may want to either host a digital-only, webinar type of set-up, or you will want to provide some web-enabled way for those unable to be present to listen in or participate. There are plenty of online tools you could Google. Your SME client, however, may simply want to create a dedicated Skype group for the event.

- Don't hand out an old-style press folder filled with fact sheet, press release, speech and hardcopy photo of the client spokesperson to every person who walks into the room. Keep a few on hand for anyone who has an equipment malfunction or has stepped in from 1989.

- It's debatable whether you need that staple of the press conference which is a formal registration area complete with A to Z displayed name tags and comely types helping you search for your name. This always results in last-minute attendees shamefully displaying their handwritten, different-from-the-rest name tags. A portable name tag maker will keep things looking professional. Alternatively, do away with the registration desk completely and simply request anyone asking a question to state name and media platform. One presentable person greeting guests at the door often works very well.

- Another good reason to dispense with name tags has to do with the habit of media houses to send junior reporters to press conferences without letting the PR agency know. So you'll inevitably have the comely ones at reception wondering what happened to Amanpour and who's that eating all the salmon? Journalists also often bring a sales colleague along for them to try and get some business on the sly. There's really nothing wrong with this. *Quid pro quo* and all that. Just make sure any uninvited advertising sales people either fall into the water feature, or don't monopolise your time, at the very least.

- As soon as the press conference starts, announce that the press release and supporting files will immediately be emailed to all in attendance. This is a great help as it means journalists and influencers can focus on intelligent questions and answers without worrying about capturing certain basic facts that should all be in the press release.

- Those present have taken the trouble to slay their morning hangovers and the traffic, and should be rewarded with a decent story. This firstly means not emailing the press release to anyone but those in attendance until at least the late afternoon, or preferably the next morning. It also means giving individual attendees a chance to speak relatively privately with the client so they can develop their own story angle separately from the herd.

- A corporate client will usually host the press conference at a paid-for venue or in the boardroom. A good tip is for smaller firms with little money and plenty to say to host an informal media gathering within the lobby, lounge or coffee area of a local business hotel. These are usually plush enough to suitably impress those attending, and management is used to meetings taking place. Obviously, don't invite more than 4 to 6 media people.

- Press conferences usually result in some of the best and most knowledgeable brains in your market being present in the same room. This is a fabulous opportunity to pick them for future story angles. Listen carefully to questions asked and statements made, write them down, and you'll have some good material to discuss with your client at the next status meeting.

- Make sure to pay any parking fees of people attending your press conference. It's embarrassing when a journalist forgets to bring change or small bills to pay for the underground parking - and you do too. You'll be forced into further awkwardness as you spend time hunting for an ATM while the journalist contemplates writing about all of this.

- Limit the stress of press conferences by convincing your client to hire a freelance photographer to help boost the media contingent with their flashy presence. A fully-kitted out photographer or videographer adds that extra professional touch to press events, particularly when you're not sure how many media people will pitch.

- One advantage of hosting a press conference at a corporate client's offices is that in the unfortunate event of the deathly silence of a virtually empty room, rent-a-crowd is easy to arrange and the few assembled guests will be none the wiser. Host the same poorly-attended PR death knell at a dedicated off-site venue and there'll be red faces all round.

7

MAKE-BELIEVE IS PART OF THE JOB

My first week of working as a junior account manager saw me introduced to a certain PR peculiarity. This is the imaginative drafting of client quotes for inclusion in press releases that are themselves largely based on the creative abilities of the PR functionary doing the nuts and bolts writing.

A big part of PR is preparing sensible written material in the client's name that is acceptable to him and is also based on your intimate understanding of both the client as an individual and of the client's company as a greater organisation with its own corporate identity and brand values.

When I was tasked with preparing my first press release from scratch, and with peppering it with quotable client quotes, I naively asked what time I could call the company spokesperson. Because I was still days into my position, and I believe the previous greenhorn had lasted two months, my boss kept her Mauna Loa on simmer and in a halting voice that suggested impressive self-control, she explained that we 'make up' press release quotes in the same way we 'make up' the rest of the press release.

At the time, I thought this was a little dishonest, to say the least, and immediately wondered about all the newspaper stories I had ever read as a dreamy child with all those wise and lofty quotes. Did Martin Luther King really have a dream? Was JFK really the one asking about you and your country?

I soon realised that there are certain indispensable timesavers in the PR industry, and proactively drafting quotes and other written material off our own bats, without any or limited initial client input, is perfectly fine, as long as the client expressly approves the final version of what you have done.

As you might have spotted, there are certain keywords in that last sentence. Make sure what the client is approving is, in fact, the *final* version and ensure you have express *written* approval (email or a screen shot of a text message) from whoever is being quoted *plus* approval from the most senior client executive you can get your hands on. This one is not always possible.

Let's go back to the creative licence issue. Obviously PR material is based on a factual premise, and excellent press releases are peppered with interesting and newsworthy nuggets of verifiable information. However, there has to be a starting point, and a big part of the PR client service game is taking the load off the client. A busy client will give you a quick Skype or cellphone brief or send you a few emailed bullet points, but it's really up to you to come up with the lion's share of written content for rubber stamping by the client.

Corporate clients can be counted upon to provide the PR firm with much more extensive briefs compared with SME clients. This is because a large amount of previously written information about whatever new product or service is being launched will already exist within the enterprise: this can then serve as awesome background information for the press release, opinion article, blog post, or whatever it may be that you are working on.

This information that will make your job so much easier could be a service description from new product development, a speech from an internal roadshow, a web copy brief sent to the advertising agency, or an internal mail already distributed to all staff to advise them of the product launch.

The rubber stamping mentioned above is actually the best-case scenario because it means you've done a great job by perfectly capturing in 400-plus words what the client wanted to say. So the approval process in these instances is simple. Just make doubly sure you always seek approval from your day-to-day contact at the client company, ideally the boss, and also from the person operationally responsible for the news you're publicizing.

In the event of changes being necessary to your written work, you need to manage the approval process perfectly or risk major repercussions. You definitely do *not* want publicity material appearing in the media without the client's express, prior approval. Getting fired is the least of your worries: in such instances, you could get sued. Sending unapproved material to the press concerning listed companies could really have serious consequences.

In the age of instant email and more web-based media platforms than we'll probably ever be able to list in any media database, you'll never be able to recall an incorrect client story like when it was a simple, yet laborious, process of calling each journalist on your list to alert them to your mistake. Back in the day, one could indeed go to the extreme of buying up copies of a newspaper you didn't want your client, his customers or business partners to see, for whatever reason.

I managed to sink to this dodgy PR tactic we've all seen featured in so many movies. Early one morning at my first PR job, my happiness at seeing one of my very first client stories appear in print soon turned to absolute horror as I realised the wrong version of the article had appeared! As luck would have it, I had arrived first that morning and all the office park's copies of that particular daily paper were neatly stacked up right before my salty eyes. I glanced at the objects of my impending doom and then at the boot of my Ford Sierra hatchback and immediately knew what had to be done. I wasn't proud of what I did but it was a relieved junior account manager who escaped intact with his many times duplicated illicit reading matter at 5pm.

Keep these approval process tips top of mind and you'll hopefully never experience the terror of the unapproved press release appearing in big, bold, fire-me letters:

- Online collaboration tools help eliminate the confusion of multiple drafts of a press release floating around.
- Never let a client verbally approve anything meant for publication.
- Any changes must be written down. Vague, verbal changes should be discouraged.
- Do not make any further changes or edits, however minor they may seem, to an approved press release or media statement. You cannot improve what's approved.
- Always try get at least two people within the client organisation to sign off releases.

- Clients love saying 'Send!'. Make sure you say 'OK!' - then wait a few minutes. I guarantee there will be times when a client's enthusiasm unexpectedly evaporates and you get a panicked phone call back: "Did you send that press release already…?!"
- Make sure your client is in the correct rational state of mind to approve media content. If something seems off, or the client is clearly distracted or under pressure and cannot properly apply his mind to the issue at hand, try hold off distribution until the following day.
- If any other companies or people, besides your client, are mentioned in the story you plan to distribute to the media, make sure they have all reviewed and approved the story.
- Even if you follow all the rules, someone one day within the client's company is going to forward the client's spokesperson a media article he's spotted and insist something is factually incorrect. You need always to have approved press releases easily at hand, with all changes highlighted and commentators indicated so you can rapidly fight this type of potentially damaging fire. You must be able to email this document to the client in a flash before things spiral out of control. It's crazy how quickly things can go pear-shaped in a corporate landscape littered with ambition, egos and agendas.

If press releases - or editorial and social content - are the engines of the PR game, then media relationships are the fuel and approvals are the ignition switches. Don't cut corners, keep each component in the system in tip-tip condition and you're in for a smooth ride.

8

DEADLINES MUST BE MET OR RENEGOTIATED, NEVER IGNORED

My introduction to deadlines began one evening during my first PR job. At a previous editorial meeting, my boss and I were each tasked with completing a story for a client's subscriber magazine. Somehow, this notoriously efficient human being (she, not me) totally forgot about the deadline between that day's angry outbursts and general, under-the-surface, volcanic seething that is typical of the Type 'A' Aries with the added loose screw.

Because she realised her mistake late in the afternoon, I reasoned I was quite literally home clear and out of the boss's clutches for another 12 hours. I naively thought we would be allowed to crank out our articles first thing in the morning. She then said something that I'll never forget: "On the day means on the day."

She insisted we both immediately sit down in front of our Windows 97 machines and work until the copy was written and it didn't matter if it was sent after close of business - on the day was on the day. We'd meet our deadline and keep our promise to the client as long as we delivered on the agreed calendar day. Some of you won't agree with this logic but it's stood me in good stead.

Even when I've slipped up and not managed to send a piece of work before close of business, I've been able to motivate myself into sitting down and at least meeting the deadline day, if not the hour, by remembering 'on the day means on the day'. Thank you,

Judy, for that one line you said in 1997. I forgive the ear-pulling. Laughing at my Ford Sierra, now that's another story!

Here are a few thoughts about deadlines, that necessary staple of the corporate world:

- Deadlines must be met. If you're a born procrastinator like me, you'll need to work on that or risk becoming a highly-ineffective agency employee or short-lived agency owner. Business is becoming very tight and that's especially so in public relations where every social media outfit and ad agency is offering to throw in PR for free. You cannot in any way afford a reputation as someone who can't be relied upon to get things done on time.

- If you can't meet a deadline, renegotiate it. Make a phone call or send an email. Never let a client deadline pass without either delivering the goods or asking for an extension. By the way, the deadline isn't renegotiated until the client says it is. So an unanswered email is no good and you'd best get on the blower.

- Don't play that corporate game and give others fake deadlines. They'll soon find out that they worked their backsides off to meet a fictitious deadline and you won't be trusted next time. You, unfortunately, are on the other side of the boardroom table so you're simply not allowed to think a stated client deadline could possibly be nonsense. You have to take your client at face value and achieve the deadlines given to you.

- You can be an agreeable Yes Person and still tell a client that a proposed deadline is unreasonable. Client service is as much about serving a client as it is about educating them about what's fair and what's not. Unless you're an airline's PR firm, you never have to answer your cellphone at 9pm. No plane is going to fall out of the sky on your watch.

- The above point notwithstanding, do make sure you're always carrying the tools of the trade (ie: a mobile device with a usable keyboard) so you can quickly meet last-minute deadlines on the fly and get back to your G&T A*S*A*P*.

9

TRACKED CHANGES CAN DERAIL RELATIONSHIPS

In the client service world, 'tracked changes' can be a big thing. For those of us who believe we write better than most, seeing our carefully-crafted press releases defaced by a cumbersome word processing feature can really make us see red. For clients, it's tempting to use tracked changes to go wild on a poorly-written press release just oozing 'lazy effort' all over those misplaced apostrophes and dangling participles.

While receiving a whole set of written changes on our work can be deflating, it's much better than receiving verbal changes. You really must encourage clients always to submit their changes in writing. Changes need to be in writing and specific, not verbal and vague.

Sometimes, PR people miss the mark entirely. Maybe it's because of the 3pm slump, or the need to hit 'send' before hitting the rapidly-approaching traffic. In these instances where you'll receive your press release back from an unhappy client accompanied by electronic snarls and nasty emoticons, it's vital to save the situation immediately by reassuring said client that all the suggested changes will be made and the amended press release will be quickly returned. Remind him of the good publicity that is sure to result from the successful distribution of the final story. Crack a self-depreciating joke.

Please never start a debate with a paying client over a bunch of silly changes. Simply hitting 'accept all changes' will save the situation and bring all emotions back down to earth. Having written thousands of press releases over the years, I know what it's like to come up with a fantastic headline, and a great angle, and then have someone crap all over your creativity. My message to you, is 'so what?'. You're either an agency owner in business to make money or you're an agency employee earning a salary. In both instances, you need to keep your eye on what's important. Making those payments at the end of the month is important. Be a Yes Person, it's profitable.

Remember that clients know best, even when they don't. Sometimes, it's so ridiculously obvious that a client's tracked changes don't make any sense. You know that by making the requested changes, the entire news angle you've cleverly come up with will be demolished and this will impact on your ability to successfully place the story. Catch 22, right? Of course not! There's another way. Make the changes in the document and get it approved. Then when you are distributing the story, gently suggest the original news angle in the covering email to your media contacts. You can generally point journalists in a certain direction, or clarify certain aspects of the press release in the introductory email.

Experienced media people will understand this is not part of the story and anything you write above the press release shouldn't be quoted. Be careful, however, as once in a blue moon, a newsroom newbie who doesn't understand 'the rules' will come along and quote you, causing all sorts of problems at inconvenient times, like first courses and last rounds.

10

PLACING YOUR PRESS RELEASE INTO THE LION'S JAW

Dealing with journalists can be intimidating because this is the closest our earthly selfs will come to interacting with an all-knowing being. Most of us who do general knowledge as a sideline can be pretty well informed. Now imagine being a professional knowledge gatherer, 24/7, and you'll have some idea of the brain with which the PR person has to contend.

All is not lost, however, because even the biggest brain has weaknesses (didn't Einstein have a well-known love for the ladies, or was that just in the miniseries?) that can be worked with for the purposes of generating press coverage for clients. When it comes to journalists, the Kryptonite of the Fourth Estate has got to be flattery, subtle of course, but flattery nonetheless. This regular and gentle massaging of media egos appeals to the reporter's all-consuming need for recognition.

Proof of this need is to be found in the terrible salaries media people are known to accept. They accept these lousy wages because there's a fabulous trade-off: they get to attach their names in black and white (or colour) to their stories. For people with lots to say to the rest of us, this is a huge plus. Media owners have noted this and not only have they historically paid media workers really badly, but they've made them slowly work their way up to what used to be the crowning journalistic achievement: the photo byline.

This is where the journalist got to attach not only a name, but an actual likeness to his work. This usually followed years of writing unacknowledged under terms like 'staff reporter'. Today, photo bylines are dished out like car allowances in a government department. What an opportunity for the PR person with a B.Schmooze degree who is left to take over the praise and recognition function.

Attempts at humour aside, it's no joke that legions of media workers are today feeling undervalued and unappreciated. Journalists could barely contend with their lousy salaries when deadlines came but once a day and they had a proven, well-defined audience that lapped up their every word. Now, realtime is the new deadline, audiences are fragmented, often unproven and no-one quite knows who's reading this stuff anymore. This doesn't bode well for very high levels of personal motivation, but it does for relationship-building.

High stress levels that need an outlet mean the PR practitioner has an opportunity to become more to the journalist than simply a source of PR puffery. Try genuinely to help out, provide support, and up your engagement with reporters, bloggers and others who write for public consumption by becoming a true 'source' - a source of encouragement, for one. Become a trusted confidant to the media worker who toils under really crap conditions while the average PR account manager eats out way more than he churns out.

Incidentally, looking on with envy is why so many reporters make the jump from journalism to public relations. While few jump back, many regret their decision after being forced to work on less-than-newsworthy stories. Straight-talking, smart journalists who know what news is, find PR client service difficult, extremely unfulfilling and a general pain in the rear.

Here are some guidelines to getting the most out of the media / PR relationship:

- When researching content to include in your press release and other written work, ensure that every fact and statistic eventually included in the final approved version of your story can be verified with a link back to the original online source. Remember to include these links in a 'Notes to Editors' section at the end of the press release so sources can easily be found. You'd be surprised how easily online sources you know were there 'just yesterday' disappear just as soon as a journalist asks a question.

- There's nothing wrong with putting a client and a journalist directly in touch with each other. Journalists will often ask for additional comment to expand on or clarify what's written in a press release. Just avoid giving out the client's mobile phone number as you don't want to create a situation where the media start calling your clients directly without involving you. Ask the journalist if he's happy to receive the client's email address instead, and then request that he copies you in any emails to the client.

- When client and journalist eventually meet in the flesh, don't be precious about controlling every aspect of the meeting. You want the media to talk to your clients, so don't get in the way and remember that you're supposed to be a facilitator more than a gatekeeper. The latter role is for the client's PA, whereas the client's PR must enable, not prevent, access.

- At the start of a new client relationship, it's worthwhile spending some time briefing the client's PA, secretary or front desk staff on the ins and outs of dealing with the media. They need to know that journalists could call them and ask to speak to the client's spokesperson. They should expect these calls and know to forward them to you, or place them directly to the designated company spokesperson, as the case may be.

- Calls from the media must always be acknowledged, prioritised and quickly acted upon. Everyone in the organisation needs to be aware that sometimes media queries will pop up in retail stores, at reception, at trade shows, at year-end parties and via the very general 'contact us' form on the company website. You would think that journalists would know exactly who to speak to at a client firm, but sometimes asking the wrong minion for a media comment is deliberate. This is why using Internal Communications to raise the profile of the company spokesperson within the organisation is often a great idea.

- When responding to a journalist's questions with approved written information, make certain you advise the journalist on who to quote. If a journalist is asking questions based on a press release received, complete with client quotes, you need to be sure he continues to quote the client spokesperson named in the original release, and not you, just because you're now emailing him additional information. I must say I loved it when my name erroneously appeared in media articles, instead of my boss's, because I knew my parents would be proud. Sadly, pleasing mom and dad is no way to run a career!

- With realtime news popping up all over the place these days, you need to clarify with journalists, bloggers and others when exactly their deadlines are. One used to know not to call journalists on deadline, but today, who knows when you could be interrupting a media person just as he's developing that last crucial thought to end off his story.

- Similarly, when responding to a journalist's emailed or phone-based questions, the first thing you do is establish his deadline so you immediately know if there's a realistic chance of a proper response from your client. If the deadline is imminent, you should try and dispense with written answers which will take the pressure off you. Rather find out if the client would agree to a quick telephone interview. If the deadline is unrealistic, you should say so.

- While you should definitely attempt to always answer a journalist's questions, in practice there is no obligation to answer each individual question as it is presented. For whatever reason, your client may prefer to respond to the journalist with a short emailed statement in response to a whole set of fishing-expedition questions.

- It is not standard practice for a journalist to share his written work with you prior to publication. He may offer to send you a draft of an article mentioning your client for fact checking, especially if it is a technical article. If so, make sure you limit your comments to the facts. Offering your opinion regarding the style, grammar and so on, is a total no-no.

- In the event of factual errors appearing in a published article mentioning your client, you have every right to ask for a correction. Please keep things polite, however, and don't use words like 'demand' because, firstly, life isn't the movies, and secondly, you don't want to burn the media bridge today you want to use to reach your client's customers tomorrow.

- Often, it is better to let a small error or two slide rather than jeopardize a good media relationship or ruin a blossoming relationship with a young reporter who'll appreciate your not making a big thing out of his inexperience.

- When a client is really upset about a publishing error, you can try calm the situation by offering such tried and tested favourites as saying it's towards the end of the story and no-one reads to the end anyway; you could mention that media platform's dismal readership figures; or you could say the error is an opportunity for further, follow-up coverage from a journalist eager to mend the relationship.

- The worst PR sin used to be not getting back to a journalist in time for his deadline. The result would be something like 'no comment was immediately received' appearing in print and the effect would be a ruined work day as both your boss and client writhed on their respective office floors while your colleagues guffawed, happy not to be that day's target. Today, the volume of email communication, in particular, I think has meant that comment deadlines are routinely missed by PR firms and their clients. The result is that audiences are now very used to seeing 'no comments' and other common phrases that hint at a PR cock-up, and largely dismiss them as part of the news website structural furniture, so to speak.

- The above notwithstanding, don't routinely miss deadlines because it's just bad form and doesn't say much about your time management - and client management - abilities.

Dealing with journalists is a definite plus when it comes to working in PR. Few ordinary citizens will ever get to interact so regularly with the people who produce the information upon which our society relies to guide its biggest decisions. Moreover, it really is a blast reading about people in the media and knowing what they're *really* like because that lovely old soak from the Daily Bugle told you so over that last six-hour 'lunch'.

11

THE ART OF THE PITCH

You don't need to know a lot to be in PR, but you do need to know a few things really well.

Top of the PR pile is knowing what makes news. You don't have to be a great writer because you can always outsource that function to someone who did have the benefit of a traditional education that prioritised certain fundamentals. A modern, liberal education really comes into its own during that annual brainstorming session, doesn't it? Pity about the rest of the year when English grammar would've been useful.

You don't really need to be a people's person. In fact, now that I think back over the past two decades, most of the really outstanding PR people I've known had what could mildly be termed as a 'personality problem'. Or, their personality was a massive problem.

This isn't the place to go into what makes a great publicist, but I'd like, briefly, to add my two cents based on what I've experienced. If I were an FBI profiler, and I met someone on the lookout for an awesome PR person, I'd advise him to search for someone with a certain angry spark in her eyes and an impatience that sees her almost permanently standing over you issuing instructions while you type (thanking God your hands are occupied). There are other attributes, but I am going to stop there out of good old-fashioned fear.

So a good publicist needs to know what's news and what isn't; he needs to know how to write - or knows someone who can write for him at a reasonable cost - and he needs either to have people skills or be so brilliant that people will forgive him for his complete lack of the common social graces that are really obvious to the rest of us. I'm talking about such basics as greeting within the confines of the elevator and allowing others to talk once in a while.

The final thing that great publicists do very well is pitch. I'm not talking client pitches where we tout for those fast-disappearing retainers, but rather pitching potential client stories to news journalists. A good PR person will be able to read a press release and summarise the gist of it in a few quick written or verbal sentences. In the 30 to 45 seconds after a journalist has answered the phone, or begun to read that email, he'll already know what the story is and why it's newsworthy enough to feature. This is because the publicist has done such a good job getting to the crux of the matter for the busy reporter.

Pitching is still carried out in person or over the phone, but selling a story today is mostly done on email or even via text or some other written social or free messaging platform like WhatsApp, for example. Regardless of the medium, the PR person still needs to be able to condense a client story down into one primary news angle that is easily explained in a sentence or two. That's the business part of it. Integral to pitching is establishing that personal connection between publicist and journalist. It's always a good idea to take the trouble to check out a journalist's most recent news articles so you can briefly mention something that interested you when you make that call or write that introductory email. Try, though, to be genuine about it, for goodness sakes: media people can smell PR insincerity a mile off.

You should also know a journalist well enough, at least after some time, to perhaps enquire about his family or mutual acquaintances. Maybe he enjoys a sport or hobby you can mention as an icebreaker in your conversation. I know this all sounds very obvious, but you'd be surprised how often the basics are ignored.

When everyone else is launching into lengthy emails without the usual salutations that used to hint at a good upbringing and relying solely on their preset company email signatures to lazily sign off emails, you'll stand out from the crowd with a little 'back to basics' politeness, and effort.

While pitching comes naturally to some born communicators, there are key pitching behaviours that can be learnt if the art of the schmooze is not exactly your thing.

When communicating with a journalist about a story you would ideally like to see the light of day, it's perfectly acceptable to play a little 'good cop, bad cop' with you - obviously - as the former and your client as the latter. While this sounds somewhat unacceptable, mildly rubbishing your client to get something good about them published is a textbook case of the ends justifying the means. Your client would *probably* understand if he caught you moaning about him to a sympathetic journo who felt he simply *had* to print your story or risk your tears making him feel terribly uncomfortable.

Emailed questions from the media following a press release from you give you some time to come up with an approved response. However, in telephone pitching you could be having a live and direct Spanish Inquisition in realtime with a highly-informed journalist. So you really need to know your stuff. Prior to making that call, read the press release or think about the proposed story angle carefully. Then come up with three to five questions you would ask if you were a media person. Write them down, do some light early-morning Googling, and get a concise set of approved answers from the client before you subject yourself to someone who knows what he's talking about.

Make sure you have the classic full colour, head and shoulders photo of the client's spokesperson to accompany the story, as well as the correct logo (there might be a specific product involved with its own logo and identity). While it goes without saying, you must impress upon the client not to send you any half-baked Facebook photos of himself. Clients should also not try and quickly erase their 'laughter lines' (now that's spin!) with some or other free photo editing app they've downloaded that morning. Warts and all, it must be. Smooth skin belongs in kindergarten, not on someone customers want to trust with their money because they think they have the experience to deliver something great.

Take the trouble to ask your media contacts when their usual deadline is. Back in the day, print deadlines were 16h00 for the following morning. Now news is constant and deadlines have evolved from pieces of string to rubber bands, if you get my drift. Multiple deadlines that stretch across an entire 24-hour day are, in fact, wonderful opportunities for the publicist. This is because we now have the ability to sell personalised stories to a myriad of journalists and have the coverage keep popping up throughout the day. In a stroke, we're now media magicians conjuring up an endless, real-time stream of coverage for the client. Before we were one-hit wonders having to constantly justify that retainer to the client, because our successful media placements were achieved only every now and again.

To me, it's as though the PR person today is packing a rapid-fire.22 machine gun, making a huge amount of small holes. Previously, the PR packed a 357 magnum revolver that punched a few really big holes. Small and often is great because it keeps the client's interest. Big and intermittent gets you forgotten.

Small and regular also looks great on month-end invoices because it's volume that wins the day. The sun set on occasional quality long ago.

12

THE ART OF THE FOLLOW-UP

The pitch and the follow-up are two sides of the same PR coin. Unless you've known your media contacts for a very long time or you're pitching a story featuring words like 'assassination' or '747' in the headline, chances are slim that anyone will reply to you, or use your story right off the bat. As you already know, the competition to get noticed is intense, and this has become even more so with easy forms of digital communication like email that enable PR people to bury journalists in mountains of unusable drivel like never before.

You can't lessen the competition or reduce the amount of emails journalists receive. What you can do is give it a fair amount of time and adopt a phased approach to the follow-up. If you sent that initial email pitch in the morning, wait at least until the late afternoon or even the next morning (you'll know what's acceptable in your market) to pretend to the journo that you forgot something in the first email. This is a great way to follow-up because you can do it in a sort of self-depreciating way that, if done skillfully, could even endear you to the hack down the end of the line (provided he's too not far gone in the jaded stakes).

You could forward the journalist a head and shoulders photo of your client, saying silly you, you're so terribly thick that you forgot to send the picture in the first email. Please don't ever ask any journalist if he's "going to use the story". Eek. That already makes my skin crawl. You have got to be smarter than trying to go through the front door.

Just send the email, resist the temptation to ask about the story, and Google a little while later to see if your story appears. For goodness sake, you need to make absolutely sure your story *hasn't* appeared before doing any media follow-ups. Don't rely on a cursory Google search because search engines are not infallible. Take the trouble to log onto individual news websites to double check whether your client's story has appeared or not.

If the story really hasn't appeared, you could try following up on a different, text-based platform. While sending an SMS or a WhatsApp message really isn't advisable (and social media DMs are totally *verboten!*), if you're desperate enough to avoid the client's wrath at the next status meeting, you may actually be driven to texting a journalist about a weak corporate story. While I am shuddering at the thought, you might simply add some minor fact that you claim to have omitted in the original emailed press release. PR is often about the lesser of two evils: angry client who pays your bills vs. angry journalist who doesn't. Remember that when you're dreading doing the follow-up with a crusty editor.

This brings me to telephone follow-ups and the fact that I haven't done one since at least 2004 when I still had an actual, stand-over-you, in-the-office boss who had to hear the industrious hum of office workers on the phone to be able to sleep at night. Today, it's almost as if telephone-based communication has been reserved for the exclusive use of annoying advertising space salespeople who really are doing an excellent job taking up the slack.

You're welcome to use Bell's instrument to follow-up with journalists about a client story. However, do so only after all other attempts at a response have failed. At least then you'll have some mitigating factors to mention when you're been bellowed at over the horn about a fast-approaching deadline (ie: Happy Hour).

Here's some more of how to follow-up without pissing-off:

- As mentioned above, first prize is a convincing reason to make contact again and visuals supporting the original written press release are ideal. A photo of the quoted spokesperson or the company headquarters, a company or product logo, or even a link to a YouTube or similar explainer video featuring the same client spokesperson quoted in the release are ideal ways to follow-up without raising either ire or eyebrows.

- Wait until the next day's news so you can purposely look out for a news article somehow related to your previous day's press release. Resend your old release and the new media article to the journalist suggesting the two might be related. Mention that there could be a story worth exploring and you'd be happy to help source any additional information required. You could even build your credibility with the reporter by offering to help out where it doesn't strictly concern your paying client. Just lend a hand for the relationship.

- Email the journalist saying the client is really keen for the story to "see the light of day" (use some euphemism that doesn't sound like you really just want your story to be published) and has therefore decided to offer said journo a personal interview so he or she can explore his or her own unique angle. This is a great one because serious journalists do not usually like to reprint the same press release everyone else is using (it is for this reason that we don't like serious journalists…a joke, of course).

- In this age of electronic mail, digital communication and mobile everything; you could really stand out by having a hardcopy press release complete with a product sample (if possible) couriered to the natural newsroom habitat of the media dinosaur who is so far refusing to take notice of your press release because "I don't print press releases". Better yet, you could drop off the release yourself. This is something to consider if you haven't yet met your media contact in the flesh. And it doesn't matter what he says about not using press releases. They all say that. Chances are reception won't allow you into the newsroom, but if you work in a smaller town, you may be able to drop your story right onto your media friend's desk (desk, not lap, please) and that's PR gold.

- If all else fails, go right back to PR 101 *circa* 1980 and try to bump into a few of the journalists, those who have so far failed to use your most recent story, at their favourite watering holes. Today, your contacts are more likely to be sipping a flat white but no matter, the concept is the same. Manufacture a media meeting. Let the journalist see that there's a real human being behind that email display name who might actually have something worthwhile to say. At the very least, you'll get smashed together and be press release friends for life! People are people and up close and personal will always trump *retina-*

display-mega-pixel-fingerprint-open-sesame-bullshit-cracked-screen-technology.

13

DISTRIBUTE YOUR PRESS RELEASES INTO A BIG BLACK HOLE

Does anything seem more at odds with the current PR focus on the creation of personalised content than the press release distribution service? The 'spray and pray' approach of yesteryear's 'PROs' was supposed to have been consigned to the dustbin of spin history along with facsimile transmission reports and press clippings that turned your fingers black.

On the surface, services where one pays per-release or fixed fees to have your press release distributed to as many as 1.7 million journalists (claimed by one firm) across thousands of news outlets appear to give credence to the perception that PR is simply about churning out press releases to as many faceless journalists as possible. The 'camel approach' is employed here - crank out so many press releases to so many email addresses that eventually one will be the straw that breaks the camel's back and something will get published, somewhere.

The above notwithstanding, there do appear to be some potentially worthwhile press release distribution services that promise somewhat more targeted distribution than the others. More than this, they claim to be able to track email open rates and more so that you'll know who is opening your press releases and where they are being published. Additional SEO (search engine optimisation) benefits are also claimed. Sounds good in theory, doesn't it?

Unfortunately, and as much as we've all tried to some extent, one cannot automate PR. Even certain aspects conducive to automation like the media monitoring function need human oversight to separate bad information from the good. In practice, the best that press release distribution services can offer is to serve as a source of background information for a journalist somewhere in the world preparing his own story. And even then, it's rare for that journalist to be working in a market relevant to your client and his customers.

You simply have to do a Google search after using one of these services to understand where I am coming from. Check the URLs of the 'news' platforms where your story has appeared and I can virtually guarantee you none will look remotely credible. The web addresses of the platforms publishing your story will typically vary from the somewhat suspect to the blatantly bizarre. Even though the entire concept of a press release distribution service is built on a flimsy premise, the acid test when it comes to the slightly more respectable services is whether it can promise placement on websites that at least look like they could be legitimate news sites with actual human beings - not bots - producing the content.

The above hints for when to use a distribution service might be acceptable. If you can find a press release distribution service that can place your stories on websites your client believes offer some sort of value, then you should use the service when you have a suspect story the client wants placed and you know none of your legitimate media contacts will use it.

I use a local distribution service in these instances and it has the added advantage of running a daily newsletter that I can also send to the client with his news snippet included. It's a great service because it guarantees one search engine result (on its own platform) that will almost always be available in cyberspace, accessible to anyone interested in my client's product category, but both my client and I know its limitations.

I should mention that the above service is completely free so it doesn't hurt to use it, and in addition it offers the two small tangible benefits described above when I'm confronted with what to do with a weak story. You should also try and find a free press release distribution service in your market. If anything, it could serve as a useful online repository of client stories.

The key in determining the potential value of press release distribution services is knowing your client. A large corporate will typically have the budget to subscribe to these services and the more established of them are not cheap. The departmental functionary making the decision will probably go for it because he's not spending his own money. Conversely, a start-up client will certainly not see the value and balk at the charges. This is because it's often the founder's own money at stake and when you're spending your own money, you're a little more careful, right? One would hope so.

Let's conclude with a little unexpected negativity, for a change! Here are three top reasons why press release distribution services might, actually, be a bit of a con:

- Very often, these services don't know the difference between who writes the stories at a media outlet and who sells the advertising space. I've seen advertising sales reps' email addresses used by these firms which is a recipe for the wrong type of returned call. When an editorial-related email address is indeed included in their databases, it's often a general one like news@acmemedia.com instead of the personal email address of the telecoms editor, for example, which is the degree of personalisation you need to get client content published.

- Most don't enable the kind of back-and-forth email or telephone-based interaction that is necessary for journalists to fact-check a story prior to it being published. Proper journalists, those who are not bots, will seldom print a press release word-for-word from a publicist or a company of which they have never heard before. Distribution services can work if the client is an exchange-listed company. In this instance, any legitimate journalist checking these services for content will know the listed firm can be trusted to prepare a factual release.

- Press release distribution services are the junk mail publishers of the media world. Unfortunately, you'll never have any degree of success with them remotely approaching the 2% mark ideally achieved by real-world unsolicited commercial mail pushers because there's far less quality control and so much more content involved.

14

MEDIA MONITORING (FIRMS) A NECESSARY EVIL

A good external media monitoring firm can provide you with the ammo you need at contract renewal time. A bad one will regularly send you advertising instead of editorial mentioning your client and argue with you about why they will continue to do so.

Here are some thoughts on why you need a media monitoring firm:

Their products have become very slick and few clients won't be impressed by the media monitoring partner's plethora of pie charts, facts and figures (and that's just their business cards!). Unfortunately, I've found that detail fatigue soon sets in after the client has signed the media monitoring contract with the third party provider. You're then stuck with a situation where no one's giving the reports much thought anymore.

In the days when all the media monitoring firm really did was courier bundles of bound hardcopy press clippings to the PR firm or direct to the client once a week, this often translated into piles of unopened press clipping folders stacked high and unread in the storeroom. Oddly enough, while I saw firsthand evidence of colleagues not bothering with the press clipping folders, it was because they were in fact pleased with the publicity effort.

They were happy to let it run because they were seeing real evidence every Friday in the form of the courier guy with the brown envelopes filled with the red clipping books. If the bundles of press clippings books had stopped arriving and the unopened stacks had not continued their steady ascent towards the heavens, then there would have been hell to pay!

Monitoring firms can be useful because you can rebrand their reports with your own corporate identity, and this will help your firm appear hugely impressive. This slapping of logos onto someone else's hard work is a tried and tested way of PR firms slotting in third-party services under their own umbrella. It's not just about taking credit, it's about making it a little harder for the client to can your services. Furthermore, these external providers are getting paid and that's why they're in business, so no one is really the loser with these little exercises in muddying the waters. Be careful, however, because when it comes to question time, the PR firm will probably not be able to answer detailed client questions about the media monitoring methodology employed, for example.

Aside from surreptitiously making their slog work appear as your own and adding reasonable 20% to 25% 'management fees' on their invoices for extra income (this is fair due to the often large gaps in your own firm getting paid), media monitoring firms can be valuable if their service includes tipping you off about breaking stories - for free. I used a wonderful media monitoring firm a while back that specialised in radio and TV. They wouldn't just send an email that was likely to be ignored or read when it was too late: their sales reps would actually place calls to PR account managers telling them about a certain story and offering to send the news or discussion item right away for a small once-off fee.

This was great because not only were developments in radio and TV covered, without the need for a long term contract, but even if you didn't order the sound bite, you could still call the client right away and let him know about a breaking story as if you had heard it yourself. Many clients must had thought we had multiple stations playing in the office all the time. I think we did, but they weren't news stations!

Perhaps the best reason to employ the services of a dedicated media monitoring specialist is so that you have some statistics or currency-based evidence of all your hard work. This is particularly useful at fee negotiation time when client and PR firm are trying to agree on a fair monthly retainer. If you can point to real evidence of millions of dollars of PR coverage being achieved, you can justly propose retainers of thousands of dollars (hundreds of thousands would be a stretch). That logic should make sense to even the most cost-conscious of clients.

Here are some thoughts on why you don't need a media monitoring firm:

With the huge majority of media outlets now having an online presence, there are few client stories Google Alerts won't pick up. My own view is that if you can get away without using an external media monitoring firm, then do it.

I find them a pain. There is too much information, too little client service and they always seem up for a fight in the event of any query. I'm generalising, obviously, but how else do you condense 21 years' experience into 115 pages? If we wanted to generalise a little further, I'd say that if you must hire a media monitoring firm, don't go with the market leader because you get a better deal and better service from the eager smaller firms.

Monitoring firms' billing is usually also a complicated nightmare and the worst is having to settle their bills on time when your own client is late paying. With these firms no longer consigned to offering simple hardcopy press clipping services, their bills can be substantial, so be prepared. And they always seem to increase month-on-month. This last point remains a mystery to me, but trust me, the first media monitoring invoice you pay will not look anything like the last one you settle.

A few final tips on working with media monitoring firms:

- Check if clips mentioning your client on certain media platforms aren't already being posted on YouTube and similar sites. If you've secured a small client that's only on media you can find on Google only every now and again, you may be able to find these mentions on YouTube, for example, without having to sign a monitoring contract.

- These firms usually ask for search terms to help them find relevant print and online articles and electronic media mentions. They'll charge more for more terms. You only need give them the company name and perhaps the name of the client spokesperson.

- Monitoring services and PR retainers are viewed by clients as one cost centre, so this means the more the client spends on monitoring, there's less of the pie available for you. This is why smaller PR firms and one-man band PR consultants try and do media monitoring themselves, with varying degrees of success.

- Make sure you work through their reports, invoices and statements with a fine-toothed comb and immediately alert them to any nonsense mentions that should not have been included and billed for. If you don't do this, you'll find their monthly fees strangely increasing as the year winds on and it won't be because of your stellar PR services.

- SME clients probably don't need dedicated media monitoring services, but large corporates most probably do. This is because when you service the latter, you will receive emails and phone calls at all hours, across all departments, requesting copies of the front page of the Daily Blah to video clips from some obscure community TV station and there's no way your time should be spend hunting down this crap. A monitoring service will easily find these mentions (that usually have nothing to with the client company and everything to do with some executive's child who won some or other talent competition or soccer match) and make you look professional at the same time.

Finally, and it *really* makes me cringe to write this, but during lean publicity times, weighty media monitoring reports containing reams of industry-related coverage can help obscure the fact that nothing much is being achieved. Terrible, but true…!

15

THE STATUS THE CLIENT FORGOT

The status meeting, usually held at the same time every week at the client's offices, is like banging your head against a brick wall - you always feel great when it's over!

But seriously, it really is like banging your head against a brick wall. And the funny thing about this, is that both clients and PR firms feel exactly the same way. The client feels nothing is being achieved and the PR firm feels like nothing is being approved. But still they meet, every week, all smiles as the list of unresolved action items on the schedule grows and grows.

Although it's more common now to host status meetings via Skype or Google Hangouts, for example, you really do need that weekly dressing down in person to keep flighty PR types on their toes. Nothing motivates me more during the working week than the thought of having to provide realtime verbal feedback the following week on each PR action item.

Aside from making sure you scrupulously list all activities you are currently working on, together with a column providing detailed written feedback for any stakeholders unable to attend status, there are about a half dozen other things you should know to help you get through your regular interrogation:

- Never be the one to cancel a status meeting. Believe me, the client wants to cancel that weekly status as much as you do, but because the relationship between client and agency is often about who failed to deliver, it's necessary to engage in a little game of 'meeting chicken'. As the minutes count down to that drawn-out weekly affair that takes everyone away from the comfort of their desks, make sure you aren't the one to blink. Be patient. More often than not, it'll be the client who phones, emails or texts to say the meeting's cancelled, just as you're about to step into the car or connect to Skype. Make sure to check your email right up to the last traffic light before the client's parking entrance. I've had clients cancel on me after 45-minute drives that saw me already in their underground parkings and lobbies. Those were the lucky times because I hadn't had to board an aircraft.

- If you're really not up to the weekly witness box session, try emailing the updated status document to the client - say your printer is down - a few minutes before you have to jump in the car to get to the meeting. Often, the client will skim through the document, be satisfied that results are being achieved, and email back to let you off the hook that week.

- Get used to the fact clients will never complete the few items in their action column of the status document. Instead of being ridiculous about it, and remembering your client service orientation, you need to help the client save face week after week by moving past his items quickly. Eventually, drop them off the list completely without anybody noticing.

- The status document should contain a summary of recent media successes achieved right upfront. This is so it's obvious to all present that the PR firm is indeed achieving on its mandate. Clients will always use the status meeting to present you with one of those wonderful bolts out of the blue when they bitterly complain about the 'lack of press coverage'. So you need to say that press coverage is right there in black and white on page one.

- Soften the atmosphere, if necessary, at status meetings with a weekly 'show and tell' you can hand, deliberately and full of smiles, to the client. All relationships, whether business or personal, go though rough patches. Weather the storm, take the edge off and break the ice - without breaking the bank - with a framed recent press story, a relevant book you thought would interest the client, or even a small gift you can say made you think of the client. 'Exhibit P.R.' can take the attention and heat off you.

- Even when you are justified in doing so, taking along unpaid invoices to status meetings is crass and a proven shortcut to eventually getting canned when the client remembers your lack of understanding and keenness to embarrass him in his own office and in front of his peers. It really is not recommended - even when your debit orders start bouncing!

- Taking along a sidekick or two is a good move. This is not just because it will afford you breathing space in difficult meetings, but because it will help you charge more by giving the impression your firm is more than just a one-man band - even when it's only a kick above in the form of a partnership of two. A lone PR consultant sitting dejectedly in the client's reception just howls 'sad' and allows the client to say, 'I can pay you less'. I have experienced firsthand the treatment one receives when you're viewed as one-man Billy versus the MD of a firm of many. Same me, different perceptions.

- Some clients will ask a minion to attend that confirmed-well-in-advance status meeting with you that clashes with some unimportant happening in their starry life. Of course, the person will have no interest in being there and this is a licence to race through the weekly action items in order to get to lunch quicker. Don't, however, let your annoyance show as the underling before you could soon morph into the overlord on your neck.

- Many clients have the somewhat embarrassing habit of interrupting the weekly status by dragging you through their building to meet and interview their fellow employees for some press release, ostensibly, to 'catch them while they're here'. It's so awkward when you're clearly interrupting people in the middle of their daily tasks. And then your client runs off to attend to another 'crisis', leaving you with someone you don't know sporting an expression that varies from the visibly uptight to the mildly perplexed. You can only get used to these hallway jaunts. They always end an hour or more later with you making your way alone, feeling like some sort of imposter, through the standard corporate maze, back to the client's office to find her happily engaged in Facebook over coffee and asking the question 'Did you get everything you needed?'. 'Yes', you think, 'Everything except a drink and a mallet…'

- Write everything down during the meeting and make sure you send the updated status document with the next action items to the client immediately after the meeting. This is a huge pain when all you want to do is hit your favourite see-and-be-seen spot for a bite to eat and perhaps a lunchtime single G&T with your pet employee. Don't procrastinate, get the amended status document out of the way, or you'll find yourself updating it an hour before next week's meeting.

Finally, and I'm not sure why this is important enough to include, but it's funny. I've noticed that many clients not only tend to eat through status meetings, but they seem to relish having an underling bring their meal to their desk while the PR firm minions huddle around the circular meeting table that comes standard with executive office furniture, like the tiny bar fridge.

My most surreal PR status meeting eating experience was watching a client's toady whip out his penknife, take out an apple from what appeared to be some sort of shared departmental fruit bowl and then slice up the fruit, handing each slice to the unflinching client in turn who ate the toady's offering in that status meeting like it was the most natural thing in the world. I never could figure out if I was being threatened.

16

MEDIA TRAINING IS NECESSARY ROLE PLAY

Media training is another one of those PR staples like the press release, the distribution list and the publicity report. However, with the last three, it's the PR consultant who squirms. With media training, you get to watch your client squirm. That's nice, for a change.

The great thing about this client squirming, is that it will ultimately make your job easier as the client becomes more at ease with being interviewed by journalists. So no more constant reassurance leading up to interviews and no fighting fires after the wrong thing has been said - on camera - for the umpteenth time, to a delighted reporter.

The websites and other marketing material of many media trainers will have you believe that media training is science. It's not. It's a few foundation tips complemented by role playing and done to the point where the client feels at ease and therefore performs better.

Confident clients make a better impression in a world where 80% of what spokespeople say is ignored. The TV viewer, for example, comes to likability and believability conclusions largely based on visual cues.

Wear a tie, speak clearly, don't get angry, smile when appropriate, thank the interviewer and keep answers brief. Don't get lost in the details and remember the value of repetition.

Is there really any more to being interviewed by the media than that?

I would add that a great way to get more for your interview buck is to try always to secure telephone-based interviews over in-studio time which is actually a waste of time. The client can reach a bigger audience with several Skype or phone interviews done from the office rather than taking the time to battle traffic just to attend a single in-studio grilling.

Counsel your clients to be careful with phone interviews, however, because that relaxed feeling that comes with answering questions from the familiarly of one's own desk can often lead to unfortunate oversharing with the journalist asking the questions.

Remind the client to keep things to the point and to remember that he is still conducting an important, make-or-break media interview, even if his shoes are removed and his favourite coffee mug is comfortably within reach.

You can reassure your client by reminding him that - in most cases - the person asking the questions is not an expert. That person is probably pulling questions straight from the press release you emailed him that morning as background. So this means the smart client can steer the interview in any direction he wants. This is a critical tip worth remembering.

Here's how to get clients to agree to media training:

- Being able to properly conduct oneself on camera or in-studio is a bona fide skill that can be added to one's resume and social media profiles. Media trainers usually record the client's training so the best mock interviews can be posted across social media as if they were the real thing, impressing all and sundry.

- The client may actually enjoy the media training to the point where he decides to carve out a more formal spokesperson's role with his current or future employers. In a world where under-pressure employers are demanding more output for the same salary, this additional responsibility could be a career saver.

- Perhaps most importantly, note that the excellent media training you have lined up will help the client's representative not look like a nervous clown the next time a journalist calls demanding live and direct answers. Nothing makes a media newbie feel more at ease than having survived that first mock media interview conducted by an over-the-hill former broadcast journalist with a surprising amount of fire left in that pot belly.

There's only one way to get the best out of media training:

- Sign up for training with one of the crusty old media farts alluded to above. There are plenty of them supplementing their pensions for the benefit of a string of ex-wives. It's perfect if they are known to have permanent hangovers to add to the unpredictability (and ultimate effectiveness) of the training. Your client should be harangued, harassed and just short of stomped on during his training. It's for his own benefit and old-school crusties are the way to go. You don't want polish, you want spit.

17

2007 WON'T BE BACK AT MONTH-END

Some clients are a pleasure. Some are a pain. Some combine the former and the latter into one irresistible package similar to the cheese and the mousetrap. Regardless of their level of fun to work with, all clients should be valued.

It's become outrageously tough out there and it's a degree of toughness our salaried and cushioned friends in predictable corporate employment will never be able to fathom. To give you an example, it's payday for most people today. That means little in one-man band agency land. What it means, actually, is that there are scarcely one or two days left in the month to achieve something real for my clients before sending them that monthly invoice. For the PR entrepreneur, month-end is crunch time, it's certainly not lunch time.

The last few days of the month are a final chance to review what's been achieved for the client and, if results have been wanting, to try and realise something meaty enough to list on that invoice you'll be sending on the 30th or the 31st. Today, we don't just increase font sizes on press releases - we're doing it on invoices as well!

I mention all of this because those happy days of fixed monthly retainers that were reliably paid each month with scarcely a grumble from the client were last seen in 2007. Today, clients want to see exactly what was achieved during the month and most want it listed on the invoice before they'll even entertain paying their PR provider. Not only this, but they also want to be copied on any communication between the PR firm and their finance department. That's how beady-eyed and on-the-money-ball most clients have become.

Most importantly, clients want to be given a choice of billing models. Many will tell you upfront that they do not pay retainers anymore. In fact, you need to make sure you never include the 'R' word in client discussions. It's no longer a 'retainer', it's a 'fixed monthly fee' - much better. 'Retainer' sounds like money for nothing. 'Fixed monthly fee' sounds like something is being delivered for the 'fee' because that's generally what happens in business when professionals charge fees. So stick with the 'f' word because this one's a good one.

If the client still does not want to pay a monthly fee, this is a wonderful opportunity for the nimble mid-sized PR outfit, or sole consultant with a toady. Your smallness makes for flexibility and quick decisions aimed at securing the potential new client. The lumbering PR behemoth with the three joint-CEOs (all called Michelle) and the redundant front desk will not be able to respond immediately to the client with an aversion to fixed marketing costs. The smaller PR concern will right away be able to offer, perhaps, a mixed charging model.

Clients obviously love results-based charging. However, before you commit to anything so complicated, know you'll disagree over what's a result and what's not. One client refused to acknowledge that any article I achieved on a certain, very respectable ICT news platform was, in fact, a 'hit' worth paying for. Others will be oblivious to just how hard you worked to achieve that single, valuable client mention on your city's leading morning radio talk show, and will flatly refuse to pay at the agreed per-hit rate.

Other clients will fuss over how many words in a news article can be attributed to them and therefore counted as positive publicity. You cannot grow a business with this type of revenue model, but in practice, you may be forced to accept this type of arrangement with a new client you're keen to land. My advice is to achieve well for the first few months and then try move over to a fixed monthly fee arrangement, making sure you keep the results up. If you slip in the results stakes, you'll be back to month-end nitpicking with the client over the tiniest attributes of the coverage you generated over the previous 30 days.

My experience has been that it is not the retainer model, per se, to which clients have an aversion - it's the feeling of being overcharged by an underachieving agency. It would seem then that offering value for money by going in with a very low retainer that keeps the long game top of mind, and consistently achieving results that are spread-out, and don't just appear at month-end crunch time, is the best way to bill those much-needed post-recession clients.

Here are some commonsense comebacks when clients spring that retainer refusal on you and suggest (almost in passing so your stunned silence will somehow mean consent) that you'll be billing them for each individual result achieved:

- Retainers are meant to protect clients from blowing their budget when the PR campaign's results start rolling in thick and fast. Be clear that the proposed retainer is actually for their benefit, not yours.

- Retainers help reduce the admin associated with managing the relationship between PR agency and client organisation. Less monthly admin means more focus on generating daily operational results.

- Retainers help motivate the PR firm to achieve results for the client. Everyone wants to be rewarded well for work well done. Predictably, the overly cost-conscious client is shooting himself in the foot because I'm prioritising the client I can count on for that fixed monthly fee over the client with the unreliable variable fee arrangement I resent.

In conclusion, we're all in business to make pounds, not pennies, and our creditors are not shy to hit us with dollars, never cents.

18

THE SERIOUS BUSINESS OF GETTING PAID

Sometimes it seems like getting paid is like getting laid because it doesn't happen often and takes a lot of effort. My wife just turned to me, dumbfounded, and said. "Whatever do you mean?" That's worrying.

It's normal for the small PR firm owner to wonder why you're in business and didn't remain in the corner office with all the advantages you never valued like always available IT support and corporate colleagues whose incompetence helped you shine easily.

As the end of the month creeps up; salaries for your one, two or three staff members will need to be paid, the greedy landlord will need to be fed, and just when you think there are a few crumbs left over for you, VAT will be due. Better yet, it will be December and the waste of space in the corner will arise from its slumber, drooling the word "B-O-N-U-S". You'll be in for a crap holiday season because presents will need to be bought with money that won't be in your account until late January.

Guess what? Some of this might be your fault. It's your fault because you let client invoices go two, three, four months past due. Being in business is all about cash flow and it needs to be consistent. Work towards a pattern where payment for work done last month is received anytime before the end of this month. While it used to be common practice for PR firms to bill quarterly in advance, that's unreasonable today. Collecting payment the month after you've done the work should be a major financial goal.

- Include a summary of results achieved on your invoices. Some late payers will attempt to query work done as a bargaining tactic. Always detailing what was achieved on the invoice is an effective way of immediately shutting down that bill avoidance avenue.

- Payment disputes (or rather, confusions) will arise from time to time. This is normal. The most important thing is not to assume you're right. It's actually safer to assume you're wrong, because that way you will preserve the relationship when the error is eventually corrected through the mature exchange of information.

- There's no point charging interest on late payments because it is just too difficult to work out. Inevitably, the client will get around to paying an old invoice and won't care that it has been resubmitted reflecting an interest amount. Don't be petty. If a regular client is paying you a fair retainer, it's ridiculous to slap on a few bucks because they're late.

- Keep the long game at top of mind. When you think in years and not in months, you won't get upset about a regular payer who is also a minor late payer. Yes, it is unacceptable that the client keeps paying in a month and a bit. But they keep paying. So don't let your anger jeopardise years of income from an otherwise good client.

- Expect that large corporates will make you jump through hoops to get paid. Just to be accepted as a supplier, you'll have to submit such antiquated documents as a cancelled cheque and a letterhead indicating your company details. Proof of tax compliance will also be required, as will a letter of good standing from your bank. The last one is always pathetic seeing as you're effectively extending the client credit, not the other way around! Most corporates won't pay an invoice that doesn't include a Purchase Order (PO) number that has been obtained before the work has been done, so don't let a client employee bully you into doing any work before they've sent you a PO number. Of course, the reality is that sometimes you will do work before you have a PO number, just to please a client. Also note that is it very difficult to explain to your typical large corporate about trading in your personal capacity, so you need to register a company to be able to invoice bigger clients.

- Something that always amazes me is how a client who hasn't paid will happily continue to demand work while never mentioning outstanding invoices. I think our Jewish friends would call that chutzpah. It's to be expected and just needs to be managed by keeping your hand under your jaw at meetings so it doesn't hit the floor. Resend outstanding invoices after new client briefings but don't threaten to stop work or you'll be shooting yourself firmly in the foot, and that always hurts at debit order time.

- If a client refuses to pay, it's usually not a good idea to go the legal route. If you must, get a lawyer to send a legal letter but it's better to use your own persuasive skills. I once wrote a nasty mock press release but I regret that moment of immaturity although it worked pretty well. If the client has valid reasons for not paying, consider offering a discount so that what's charged matches the results delivered. Invoices are not carved in stone and you'll make it up in the long run by retaining the client.

There are two words that easily sum up all of the above: Be reasonable. Client memories tend to sharpen at contract renewal time.

19

HOW TO BE A SUCCESSFUL POT PLANT

Pot-planting is necessary if one is to progress in one's career. This is especially true if you work for a large corporate where your boss has unlimited funds to throw around to make herself look good. It's not so much a requirement if you work for yourself where you hope the client has outsourced the standing-around-at-events function. Let's rewind a little.

Pot-planting, for the uninitiated, is when low-level eventing employees stand around trying to look awesome while pretending to themselves that an entire event depends on them. The whole idea is that they should blend into the background while not letting their ridiculous FBI headsets frighten the guests. Pot plants always wear black. And comfy shoes.

To be fair, events do depend on lots and lots of pot plants getting things right. They must not let gravity get the better of them. They must know when to point left or right, and they must be familiar with standing upright - at least when other people are clothed. They must also look awesome. And master that tricky business of looking serious / professional rather than serious / unfriendly.

At some point, your boss is going to ask non-pot plants like you to be greenery for an evening. It might be a company awards evening, the chairman's birthday or whatever. The reason doesn't matter because the point is, you've been asked and you must. My ridicule above should not detract from the basic fact that pot-planting is a great opportunity for the young PR person. You should not be a Prima Donna and act like you're too good to stand around bored out of your mind while other people wish they were at home in bed with the dog.

The truth is most of the guests will be bored too. But they'll be important people who might notice you as they scan the room for the resident hottie. There's always one, never two.

This could be good for your career later on because the fact you were at Glitzy XYZ Event could be the ice breaker in the lift that goes all the way to the top floor. Most importantly, just being at a VIP function, in whatever capacity, means you already have one up on your colleagues who weren't asked to pot plant because they were either not presentable or not bright enough - it could only be one or the other.

Here's how not to mess up your pot-planting debut:

- Don't let anything pass your lips during the entire event. That means no eating the food, no drinking the bottles of branded water and definitely no standing around smoking with the herd. If you want water, go to the bathroom and drink out the tap - discreetly.

- The quickest and most discrete way to exchange contact details with any potentially useful bigwigs you might meet is with the good old-fashioned business card. Make sure you can get to yours quickly. Your boss won't be happy if she spots you currying favour with the next rung on her ladder.

- Practise the art of standing out while fitting in. You want to be the one approached by the lost VVIP with whom you can spend a few precious minutes escorting to his seat or car. You don't want anyone to think you actually tried to be the chosen one. That makes for fairly unpleasant next day mornings in the open plan. Whatever you do, please don't get in the car. That's the quickest way to getting that PA, Business Development or Head of Pot Plants 'promotion' and simultaneously the best way to write off your eventual better future somewhere else.

- Unfortunate things always go down when a forest of pot plants winds down post-event. As tempting as it may be finally to stand a chance of getting to grips with a colleague's topsoil, you really do not want to be around when the obligatory few drinks turn into invoices for damages being sent to your company. Try and stick to this rule of thumb: when your boss leaves, you wait five minutes then also leave. And make sure you send her a message wishing her a safe drive home and assuring her that you're also on your way home. That way she knows to leave you out of the inevitable post-event disciplinary.

A great example of a post-event disciplinary I probably shouldn't share involves one of South Africa's leading ICT firms, a newly-installed executive, a pond, lots of alcohol, few clothes and his first company function (he was nervous). The long-term implications were profound - he never drank again and the Koi lost their home.

By the way, pot-planting may be low level, but only the best with the most potential get to swim in the pond.

20

BRIEFING BY BMW

Amongst the typical client behaviours that account-facing PR people everywhere must get used to is 'briefing by BMW'. This simply refers to the common tendency of clients to call you when they're nice and snug in the car, stuck in traffic and at a bit of a loose end.

So who do they call but the person paid to listen and to dispense sound advice? You must expect client calls during the early morning and late evening peak hour traffic times. Try and be settled already and have your coffee in front of you, particularly on Monday mornings and Friday afternoons. This will perk you up enough to be on the ball and able to provide a good sounding board for whatever ails your client at a particular turnpike.

A client calling from his car (he should have pulled over, but we'll settle for bluetooth-based road safety instead) for a rolling, good-humoured, folksy kind of chat is the best case scenario. Unfortunately, clients have a tendency to call you when they're all het up because someone else has called them from their own car following one of two things.

This person, who is usually an unnamed relative, has heard something vaguely related to the client's business on his car radio or he has seen something of interest on a passing billboard. Now he's calling his big-cheese C-level relation to let him know.

You would think that this informal media monitoring service provided by the client's hangers-on would be a useful thing. It would, but sadly the CEO's friends and relatives (and even the client) usually get these radio, billboard and poster alerts really badly wrong. Sometimes, someone calling to alert the client to a relevant radio interview, for example, that he's carefully paying attention to and that is indeed of interest, can really be a good thing. This is particularly true if you haven't heard the interview or news segment yourself. This is valuable because you can immediately leap into action and perhaps call a producer to offer the station an interview with your client or send a background press release on the company for the next time the topic comes up. Great.

Unfortunately, and maybe it's due to excessive traveling speed, but a client calling from a car to relay information from someone else in a car, usually ends up with the publicist embarking on (another) wild goose chase. Stations will be confused, names befuddled and broadcast times massively messed up. Trust me, you'll never find that interview segment the client's third cousin twice removed insists he heard 'not five minutes ago, Ivan…'.

This exact scenario happened to me this very morning, just prior to my writing this installment of PR wisdom. Luckily, my beautiful baby twin girls have been doing a CNN on my wife and me for the last few months by waking us every hour on the hour. So I was awake, full of coffee and theoretically functioning at the conscious level at my desk when one of my clients called just after 7am. Not too early, but did I mention it's Monday today?

He was mildly upset, to say the least, by the actions of a large state-owned enterprise that had done something unexpected and untoward concerning a tender involving the client's company. He was adamant he had seen a headline to this effect on a newspaper street pole poster while driving to work. He demanded that I immediately knock out a media statement, email it to him for approval within a few minutes, and then send it to 'everyone'.

In these situations, you have to get the client to hit pause and rewind. Without pause and rewind, you'll be fast-forwarding to a massive publicity disaster. After listening to the client for a few minutes - and not finding anything remotely related online while I listened - I calmly suggested we go back to this offending street pole poster. Surely, others must have seen it, so would he allow me to jump into my own car and go in search of it? I knew that would buy us a little time that would enable the client to start seeing things in perspective.

Needless to say, I couldn't find the poster. To double check, I called a couple of friends I knew would also be on their way to work in the same city as the client. I'm in a different town, but it shouldn't have mattered as the newspaper is a national business broadsheet.

The client I spoke to later sounded like a different person. He realised he had come to the wrong conclusion after the briefest of glances at a flapping poster in the near dark. Now imagine if yours truly had trotted out a strongly-worded media statement about a make-believe news item! Pause and rewind. Go back to the source of the excitement to calm things down. Never proceed without tangible confirmation that you can plainly see yourself.

When you're being 'briefed by BMW' by an irate executive you reasonably believe to have gotten the wrong end of the stick, you have to hold onto the reins of the bucking client, let him ride himself out, and when he's calmed down sufficiently, propose a conservative plan of action that should involve buying time until things become clearer.

The good news in all of this is that after a tremendous amount of excitement, the client will usually forget all about the call to you the moment he drives into the underground parking and spots his new PA.

21

THANK THE PR GODS FOR GOOGLE

Google is the most significant development to hit PR land since the press release. While most of us would be familiar with Google as a search engine, the mere fact that you know about this phenomenal company and its self-driving cars illustrates that things have really moved on since you first Googled what Google meant. That's when you discovered that 'Google' is a misspelling of a real-life mathematical term, googol, which is 10 raised to the power of 100.

Although Wikipedia describes this US firm as a 'technology company', PR people everywhere are beginning to appreciate its real value (at least to us) and that's as a publisher. Forget self-driving cars and other indulgences of the cash-rich corporation: Google is quite simply the biggest publisher of content the world has ever known.

In my experience, clients - especially the small to medium-sized ones - are mostly concerned with two questions when it comes to PR. "What's the value of PR?" and "Where did my story appear?". More about the first one later, but the mere fact the client has engaged your services probably means he's answered the first question himself.

The second question hints at the client's reasonable expectation that the press releases you prepare for him should, in fact, appear in or on some legitimate digital or traditional news platform. While the expectation is reasonable, for many of the people reading this book, most of us will work on clients engaged in less-than-earth-shattering activities much of the time. Profiling big corporates in the media is a total breeze. For one thing, journalists call you! When I worked in the corporate affairs department of South Africa's leading cellular network, there were so many incoming media calls that it simply wasn't necessary to trawl proactively through media lists on a daily basis to try and get something published.

Coming from a small PR agency where as a junior account manager I had to work on profiling such embarrassingly inconsequential stories in the community press as a local firm sponsoring soccer balls, for example, it was a surreal experience to do very little to get a story into the media. Vodacom was spending millions on building schools, police stations and clinics - at Nelson Mandela's request. How easy is that PR?

It's with the smaller clients that you really have to put on your thinking cap. They'll call you, all breathless and excited, about some niche product only of interest to a tiny group of people in some far-flung corner of the country and expect a front-page story. PR is about managing client expectations while also being enthusiastic about the news and trying your level best to get that news placed. Enter Google.

Do try your damnedest to get your client's wife's latest charitable endeavour into the social pages of your city's biggest daily newspaper. However, when you manage instead to achieve a semi-respectable placement within an important local blogger's weekly round-up of feel-good news, you absolutely must communicate an important fact to the client. Your success in communicating the following piece of common sense will determine your future relationship with the client. You want him to remember this when he thinks of you.

The actual news platform is less important now: what counts is its search engine availability. In other words, you want to be able to type in a relevant search term on Google and for the client's story to appear. Does it really matter which platform is hosting the story that is now searchable and findable to the world because of your PR efforts?

Of course it does matter a little, but not as much anymore. This is especially true when it comes to smaller clients who are more interested in results over ego. Most SME clients are just wanting to see visibility that'll add some value to their entrepreneurial endeavours. They're looking at what's being displayed on the page when people click on that first search result - they're not looking too hard at the URL displayed within the browser.

Obviously, the source doing the hosting adds some credibility, but that's mostly true if the platform is a top-tier BBC or a CNN, or whatever your local equivalent is. Most of the rest blur into one media fog. Sometimes you do want to reach a critical audience who you know consumes a particular media platform. Most times, however, you just want the story out there, somewhere, so it can reach critical mass, or become part of a greater narrative.

Tell the client that the mere fact that his story is now permanently available in cyberspace, to anyone who searches for his name or company name, now and in the future, is huge. What you're doing as a publicist is helping your client build a corporate history on the global repository of forever information that is the worldwide web.

I've heard the most difficult of clients go silent on the other end of the line as he carefully considers this reasoning. It really resonates with people because it's so true. Just get your client's stories out there on the web and don't care so much about the platform that's doing the publishing, because the engine that's doing the searching is much more important.

What could be more conducive to future growth than helping your client lay down successive layers of solid corporate information, year after year? There are many benefits to this. When it comes time for your client to exit his start-up, for instance, prospective buyers will be impressed by all the search engine results they see going back years. All of this will be due to you.

So build this Google-related, PR permanence into your pitches, and try and skirt the issue of PR measurability as I have tried to do here!

On measurability, my experience is that it is large corporate clients who are obsessed with measuring the financial value of PR exposure. Smaller clients that are owner-managed will instinctively know when they are getting PR value and when they are being taken for a ride by their PR firm. Because they can afford to, let the enterprise-class clients go ahead and throw their money away by contracting with an outside measurability partner that will provide oodles of doodles that look awesome and have no real effect on your PR activities.

22

CONNECTIONS, GOOD OR BAD, ARE STILL CONNECTIONS

The land of press releases and dragon bosses is a small place. Without wanting to jinx your current meteoric rise, you would be wise to remember that the people you tread upon on the way up, are the very ones who will pee upon you on the way down. If you can't do it for the right reasons, think of being nice to clients, co-workers and others as a kind of career insurance policy. It'll pay out in so many varied ways when you least expect it.

I remember a very heated discussion with a Zimbabwean colleague involving land invasions around the year 2000. I always made an effort to understand his views and eventually we were on the same page. In 2016, I secured a new client and the marketing director invited me into his CEO's office. Guess who was seated behind the desk?

It has been enlightening to say the least to witness people I met in my early 20s as a very green agency PR account manager in Cape Town, and then as a somewhat more experienced corporate PR manager in Johannesburg, gravitate to all kinds of interesting positions. Those were the lucky ones.

Don't ever think that, just because you knew someone as a top-flight career executive, he'll always occupy the corner office and the double parking bay, and have power over you. Too often, life happens and careers go off the rails. Conversely, divergent opportunities can also present themselves and a promising new life will begin.

I've seen a financial manager turn his hand to craft brewing, a risk management executive turn crazy, a C-level inspiration have his career cut short by coronary challenges, and most importantly for the purposes of this discussion, I've experienced complicated 'frenemy'-style relationships turn into old-fashioned friendships. This usually happens when one matures to the point where people around you start dying and you realise that even frenemies are to be valued. So expect that around 40 you'll be inviting some surprising choices to tea!

With the above in mind, what follows is a really great piece of advice. The mere fact you know someone right now is more important than your past experience with them. Huh? I believe I have actually confused myself with that clumsy line I just can't seem to get right.

What I am trying to say is that when you come across an old colleague, or anyone for that matter, and you've had conflicts or an ongoing issue with them in the past, when you bump into them in a different context some time later, isn't it true that - in most cases - there'll be smiles on both your faces and a genuine happiness to see each other? I've certainly found that. It made me understand that this is why we 'let bygones be bygones'. That former negative interaction has, oddly enough, served to form a weird bond between the two of you that can now be exploited as a commonality to get you both moving forward and achieving together on some new venture.

Here are some hints and tips for the start-up agency owner, the agency employee and the corporate worker at the PR coalface to think about when it comes to the people we meet in the course of our careers:

- Focus on making your circle bigger, not smaller. Draw more people into your circle of influence. Remember to get their contact details and add them on social media. Don't cast people out.

- Even if you fall out with some people, don't write them off completely. Follow their careers and keep tabs on them from a safe distance. One day, the time may be right to reconnect.

- When you meet common acquaintances, ask after X and Y frenemy. Word will get out and this will help mend relationships in the future. Enquiries signal that peace is coming.

- Recognise that human beings have limited attention spans, time and resources. Different people are important at different life stages. Don't write people off. Rather park relationships, mothball feelings and rediscover connections at a later stage when the PR stars align.

23

A KIND WORD FOR THE CLIENT

It's a terrible fact of PR life that so many agency employees slag off the client just as soon as the weekly status meeting ends and the elevator doors close.

I remember being horrified, as a young 20-something, to hear my colleagues rubbishing the client employees they had just a few minutes earlier been schmoozing with a degree of enthusiasm that would make a 1970s-era used car salesperson blush.

I drove home in my 1980s-era metallic blue Ford Sierra thinking what a shit I was for not speaking up. When I got home and rewarded myself with a glass of sparkling wine and a pie for having achieved my first salaried job, I thought about it and realised I was raised too well to copy my colleagues' bad habits convincingly. Even back then, it was patently obvious to me that clients were customers and we were fortunate to have them.

You should work hard to cultivate a genuine appreciation of, and even affection for, your clients. They may blast you with a harsh word now and again, but if you do your job right it should only be now and again.

To the external consultant who only sees the client in the flesh once a week or less, it may seem like his job is a breeze. After all, you do all the work. Not really. While you work for a small agency, or on your own, the client has to contend with the stressors of corporate life and they're significant. From brown-nosing to xenophobia (I kid you not), and traffic, the corporate employee does not have it easy all the time. It's your job to support him and to do it in a way that makes both you and your client happy.

Should you eventually go down the route of starting your own PR agency, you'll realise that not only is making nasty comments behind your client's back common and rude, it's horribly ungrateful. Of all the legions of PR people in the country, the client has selected you. Their monthly retainer that is regularly deposited in your bank account pays for everything in your life from prescription medicine that keeps you ticking to the roof over your head that keeps you dry. It really is a sign of low breeding to speak ill of your customers. Clients are customers at the end of the day and you'd best remember it. Did we mention they're people, too?

24

THE SHITTY CLIENT

Who doesn't love the client who pays on time, and is kind to boot? Unfortunately, once in a blue moon, you'll have to service the kind of client who just wants to give you the boot! This usually happens when the day-to-day operational client is a marketing functionary and is forced to work with you because 1) you do a good job 2) you're affordable 3) you're affordable.

These types of clients are usually a new hire within the marketing, corporate affairs or PR department and come with their own relationships and connections from their previous job. They'd like nothing more than to see the back of you so they can bring in their PR buddies from the last job they cocked up. Unfortunately, as the likely scenario goes, your longtime friendship with their MD makes that impossible. And, boy, do they resent you for it.

For your part, you'll begin to resent driving to status meetings that begin to blur into one endless succession of long faces. You'll start getting seriously upset when you see the client's switchboard number making its umpteenth appearance on your mobile as the new hire swamps you with last-minute tasks designed to see you fail.

Each time you answer in your usual upbeat client tone, there'll be that deliberately emotionless shit on the other end of the line who couldn't be bothered to greet you properly. Do not give up, even if it's just for the satisfaction of seeing her fail first.

Herein lies the key. You just need to outlast this cretin. Very often the kind of person I am trying to describe here has been through a succession of recent positions that probably lasted from six months to two years. Just hang in there and give them plenty of rope to hang themselves.

So what to do about it? Here are a few proven tactics:

- Do your best. If you deliver a great service, you'll feel less anxious because you'll know any friction in the relationship is out of your control and not due to shoddy PR work.

- Try to connect with Grumpy Guts. The best way is to get her out of the office by going for a long sunny afternoon lunch on neutral ground. A good idea is to treat her where people really do know your name. This way, she might begin to see you as an actual human being she can work with. Ply her with a few drinks and see if you can't establish some mutual connection.

- If all else fails, keep in there with the big boss.

- Finally, don't pull out all the stops because it won't help retain the client. Huh? This one may seem at odds with the first point above but it's not. Do your best, but don't go overboard by putting your life and soul into this one client. There's a fairly good chance that the new client hire who wants you gone will succeed, eventually. Because of this, you don't want to have neglected your other clients who aren't total shits by trying to please this one total shit.

25

STAYING CLEAR OF THE BULLSHIT BRIGADE

In the eighties and nineties, every slippery-tongued bullshitter worth his last bounced cheque claimed to be into 'import / export'. Today, every second restaurant tap water sipper and bar drinks scrounger is a 'businessman'. Businessmen used to be known for suits and ties and actually getting up in the morning. Popular culture now credits every cretin in a tracksuit with nowhere to go as a businessperson. That pisses me off as a small business owner who's earned his stripes through consistent toil over twenty years.

The problem for you as an up-and-coming PR business owner, or account-facing agency employee, is that your obvious work ethic and switched-on nature will attract these self-styled 'businesspeople' at a rate you never imagined. They'll begin to notice you whacking out a press release on your mobile device at your favourite restaurant or stepping out to take an after-hours client call at your local bar. Their heart rates will accelerate at the thought of potential freebies as they take you for a soft-hearted type who always pays his way. This advice will save you years of annoyance and a ton of cash. Learn how to be abrupt, practise cutting conversations short and study the science of invisibility.

You know how they say you'll never pick up anyone worthwhile in a bar? Well, that also applies to potential clients. Don't try networking with strangers after dark with alcohol involved because all that will happen is the local bullshit brigade will rope you into some crazy scheme that has you doing all the work for no money. Word will get around that you're the go-to media person, and every slippery turd with no cash will try get you to promote his latest disaster with promises, promises, promises. At first it's a lot of fun to walk into some establishment after work and have a host of people yell your name as the high-fives fly. When you're under 30 you feel special. When you're above 40, it becomes irritating because you finally realise every high-five will cost you money.

When I rented an office in Parkhurst, Johannesburg, the scenario I've described above became so bad that I could not walk down 4th Avenue without collecting a retinue of hangers-on that typically included a few car guards asking for accommodation and loans and a couple of 'businessmen' asking for accommodation and loans. Strangely, I never had any good-looking PR 'Michelles' (why are they so often called Michelle?) asking for accommodation, just loans. It is vitally important that, as you build your PR business or progress in your PR job, you do not allow big talkers to distract you with promises that will never be fulfilled. You must learn to separate potential clients from potential headaches.

Stay focused and don't spend your limited time on this earth with the likes of these:

- Namibian national X wasted hours of my time over many months talking about his DRC mining operations and capped it all with a request that I deposit R200 in my office postbox because he could not afford to buy groceries. Of course I did. "There but for the grace of God go I," and don't you forget it.

- Madame Y flashed around a 16-page CV listing her dubious qualifications, never paid any PR invoices, would routinely pilfer cookies (seriously), and is on television today dispensing advice to a believing audience.

- Small business commentator Z speaks on mass media platforms about how important SMEs are to the country, and yet his last monthly PR invoice for three media articles achieved and two lengthy newsletters written remains unpaid since 2011. The shit.

26

KEEPING UP APPEARANCES

Hands up who likes meetings? Amazingly, some of you actually put your paws up! Well, I don't like meetings. And I dislike status meetings, in particular.

Like many results-driven publicists who run their own small PR agency, I feel that the weekly suction session takes me away from the comfort of my desk and the motivation provided by my hourly Americano. It totally and completely prevents me from cranking out proper results for my clients.

Every minute spent in traffic, parking in the client's underground bunker meant for little European tanks, signing in at a reception designed for would-be criminals on the honour system ("are you carrying a gun?") and thinking of the usual ice-breaker in the lift, totals up to hours wasted.

When I first started out in PR in the Late Medieval Period, we used to write press releases by smashing rocks against giant Redwood trees. No, that was (the late) (bastard) Max Clifford's time. I remember now that the standard way of getting things published in my early 20s was to fax a covering letter accompanied by a one or two-page press release in the correct spacing to dozens of journalists and editors.

The fax numbers were all pre-programmed into Ye Olde Facsimile Machine and while the thing was slowing spitting out its black-and-white PR waffle on the other side, we would telephone every person on the list to 'sell' them the story, offer them follow-up interviews, ask if they needed a photograph to accompany the story and generally give our client a good punt. Of course, you also needed to be interested in the journalists' lives, giggling along with them about their heavy drinking and asking if it was 'time' yet…

So, this actual speaking to actual human beings was how PR was done back in the day. Then email came along and changed everything. Suddenly, whole back and forth 'conversations' were possible without an insincere publicist ever talking to an intoxicated journalist. Media people everywhere celebrated. Cheers. Bottoms up.

Seriously, this all made me feel very guilty. I loved email because I hated making those follow-up calls. I felt they must be so intrusive to any journalist trying to concentrate between hangovers. It just didn't seem right that client stories would appear in the media without any real interaction between the PR person and the journalist. I soon got over this.

Technology, and mobile technology in particular, has indeed changed the PR game forever. You need to be careful, however, because there is a definite requirement to put in personal appearances now and again. In the long run, you cannot get away with running a PR account remotely from the comfort of your coach, or the beauty of the beach. No way.

As a current small agency owner keenly aware of my monthly operating costs, it's very tempting to cancel that monthly flight to the big city to meet my clients. I know they'll be okay with an emailed status update and, of course, they will - in the short term.

But for so many reasons, one cannot sustain a long distance PR relationship without the regular up close and personal meeting. While it may seem unproductive, seeing your client in the flesh is the most productive thing you could be doing with your time. It'll be during these contacts that the real bonding between client and PR will take place. That helps tremendously at invoice time.

- Arrive for your big city meeting as if you belong there. If you've relocated to sunnier climes, don't arrive looking suntanned and wearing anything remotely leisure-related. It just doesn't go down well.

- Definitely don't arrive at any meetings with a ton of luggage. Take the earliest and latest possible flights so you can get there and back in a day and don't have to take any heavy bags.

- After the meeting, don't walk out the building with your client and let him see you waiting on the corner for an Uber. Somehow, it just looks unprofessional. Don't even think of asking for a lift.

- If you're doing the there-and-back-in-a-day run, take your own coffee and food to save time and money. You don't want to be hunting for snacks and standing in queues when precious minutes are ticking by. Also take plenty small bills. Card machines *will* be down.

Doors to manual!

27

NEVER GIFT AN UNFORTUNATE HORSE

Slavishly exchanging gifts is a big part of business, is it not?
While it certainly used to be, recently-enacted corruption-busting
legislation across the globe has practically criminalised the
innocent giving of expensive and undeserved gifts to company
representatives.

How infuriating for the publicist who only wanted to present the
six-figure client with a bottle of four-figure whisky because he's
such a nice guy. The company man, not the PR. It's a pity that
states had to go so far as to enact complex legislation in the face
of the willy-nilly dishing out of the odd helicopter to hardworking
rubber-stampers.

All respectable national governments had to do was take a page
out of their own media's book. Reputable publishing houses have
for decades had in place simple and effective policies when it
comes to individual journalists receiving gifts. In many towns and
cities countrywide, PR people are clear that any gift to a reporter
at the Sunday Times, for example, will immediately be returned if
it is valued at over a certain amount. If it is judged to be under
that amount, it will likewise not be retained by the journalist for
his own use, but be placed into a common pool to be auctioned
off once a year for charity.

This is a wonderful way for a media house to manage the
potentially thorny issue of gifting by PR firms. I love the
charitable angle and the downright simplicity of it. It's great that

the PR firm's gift is, in fact, accepted. It's just that it will end up benefiting someone even more unfortunate than a journalist.

The message here is for publicists to be aware of gifting policies in their own markets and to understand that even if an inexpensive gift is kept by a reporter, their editor would have to give them the go-ahead to drink it on their own time. Remember media gifting policies when dishing out pressies at glitzy events where what's included in the take-home bags can really get out of hand. This could necessitate a separate media registration area.

The emergence of the semi-professional blogger has created some confusion amongst publicists when it comes to what's acceptable gifting practice and what's not. This is especially true when dealing with bloggers and similar quasi-'journalists' who have received no formal journalism training. You can be sure they never wrote a 70-page dissertation on ethics, and isn't Gutenberg that really hotshot divorce lawyer?

Many of these aspiring media personalities are running mildly-successful platforms with little or no advertising support and are therefore quite happy to accept any gift with some monetary value that can help reduce their expenses; food and entertainment or otherwise.

I remember being quite taken aback, at first, when trying to generate coverage for a top-end new restaurant across a range of lifestyle blogs. Many of the website owners dispensed with any pretense of politeness and practically demanded food and drinks vouchers, of substantial value, before they would run any story about the new venture.

Obviously, one understands the need to sample the wares before writing about what's on offer. However, can the same be said when you're a design blogger?

There are tools available on the web for estimating the traffic of many websites. While their accuracy leaves a lot to be desired, like polygraphs, I'd still advise any publicist to run these traffic tools when confronted with a blogger suspiciously too big for his boots.

Many blogs can be dismissed - with contempt - as nothing but freebie touting tools for the entitlement brigade short of enough passive income from their last Divorce, Inc.

Last but not least, here are four client gifting considerations:

- Gift one year and you'll be forced to continue gifting into perpetuity or risk your client wondering why the relationship changed.

- We live in a multicultural world full of strife, bigotry and misunderstanding. Try to lessen that last one by appreciating that fine booze, for example, is best gifted to close friends and family whose religious, political and other persuasions you can reliably guess.

- On the necessity of gifting, especially in tough economic times, ask yourself if adding another exquisite non-essential to someone's bi-annual (birthday and the year-end formerly known as Christmas) pile is really, truly going to help you retain that client.

- Don't bother sending a donation in the client's name and calling it a gift. I don't know anyone who's ever been over the moon knowing money that could've been spent on him has gone to an endangered lizard, a starving pooch or an unfortunate horse.

Finally, my wife typed this chapter because I cannot bear the term 'gifting'.

28
"EN ROUTE"

Popular culture belittles the 'Yes Man' but why are you in public relations if not to accede to client requests? One of most important attributes you can learn in business is the ability to pipe up enthusiastically: "Sure, I'll get it done!". If you can cultivate a reputation as the go-to person when others can only think of excuses, then you've already won half the battle.

This brings me to something I just could never get my head around during status meetings when my employer Vodacom was the client and one of the PR firms that rates itself so highly was our retainer agency. Every week it would be the same predictable game where our Corporate Affairs executive would ask the agency for something and the Account Director would take off her glasses and rub her faulty slits while explaining in so much detail why Easy Task X could not be done. Or, if it could be done, it would cost more and take forever. Why longer? The agency would simply outsource and add a juicy mark-up.

Usually, however, she would use the standard PR excuses that are always so amusing because these same flimsy lines have been trotted out for eons. I guarantee you David slew Goliath on a Friday just before lunchtime but the news was delayed because the PR guy said no one would be at their chisels until Monday morning. There was plenty time. He just couldn't carve out a press release AND make it to the taverna for an early amphora.

Another classic excuse when the PR firm doesn't feel like doing too much work in a particular week is to claim that next proposed press release will 'swamp the media'. That's because your 'ubiquitous' and 'innovative' product is so earth-shattering that news of it will surely send the country's thousands of journalists completely over the edge. "That's it!", they will cry, "We're swamped. Oh, the humanity!". Inevitably, Easy Task X would be given to internal media person Ivan, earning the scorn of the PR agency charging a six-figure retainer. Per month. In 2004.

The problem with being lazy - because that's what coming up with excuses really is about - is that you can only say no to your client a limited number of times, or drop the ball, before you receive that email assuring you that it's not you they are unhappy with, it's the economy. The problem is, it is indeed you that's messed up. The client has simply weighed up what you are being paid, either as an agency or a one-man band, versus what you've been achieving each month. The answer he's come up with is, well, not in your favour. And the best way to avoid a fight, is for him to smile sweetly while he's planting his foot firmly on your backside.

This happened to me when I didn't truly appreciate how fortunate I was to receive a good amount of money each month for doing a relatively simple task that almost came naturally. In fact, it happened a few times. However, I am pleased to say it hasn't happened for many years because I grew up.

The purpose of this installment of PR wisdom is to appeal to you not to make a career of making excuses. As times become tougher, as competition becomes greater, the excuse will not wash. It's yesterday's PR tactic and believe me, it was a tactic commonly employed because it bought time. You used to be able to get away with "the press release got stuck in my outbox" routine. Today, your client will simply ask you to re-send it right there in the meeting. Therefore, to avoid red faces all round, just do the work. It is so much easier.

And the reason this chapter is called 'en route'? Well, I have a wonderful friend who hates me. He must hate me because he will keep me waiting at an appointed venue, at the appointed time, and not show up for hours. To every location-related question, I will receive an 'en route' message. I'll go home, fall asleep and wake the next day to many of these. I've joked with him that I will put 'en route' on his headstone!

Making excuses is a counterproductive business because you buy a little time for a lot of stress. The excuse to time exchange rate is just dismal. It's horrible to deny the existence of email after email, to dread the sound of the ping. With acceptance comes happiness, so accept that you're in a service business. You simply must agree to do things, on time, without uttering embarrassingly transparent excuses that will eventually demolish your reputation first and your bank balance second.

Don't be the one who is always 'en route'. Be already there.

29
ENDS

Thank you to those readers who started on page 1 and read all the way through to page 115. To those of you who flipped straight to page 115, well done. You truly have what it takes to be a top PR achiever. Drop me a line at booth.ivan@gmail.com to let me know who you are.

I've enjoyed writing down many of the things I've learnt over the past two decades in PR. I wanted this book to be a bespoke PR compass, not a mass-produced PR GPS. Does that make sense? It does to me and it will to the reader I had in mind while writing these pages.

Anyone can Google how to compose a tweet. This book wasn't meant to replicate reams of 'how to' advice easily found on the web, but rather to provide unique operational PR insights that haven't appeared elsewhere - with a dose of humour to help it all go down.

A final thought is to remember that the majority of PR clients will be very happy as long as you are regularly sending them tangible examples of coverage you've generated.

Be proactive and creative with story angle suggestions, write up agreed angles quickly, place the approved press releases on legitimate platforms, email clients the coverage links and remember to list these results on your invoices. Do all of that and you should retain clients long enough to secure that buy-to-let second home you always dreamt would free you from the tyranny of the press release.

The best of luck to you.

IVAN BOOTH

www.ingramcontent.com/pod-product-compliance
Lightning Source LLC
Chambersburg PA
CBHW060617210326
41520CB00010B/1378